TURTLE DESIGN IN A RABBIT AGE

Mindfully Crafting Your Meaningful Life & Brands

TURTLE DESIGN IN A RABBIT AGE

Mindfully Crafting Your Meaningful Life & Brands

by Mel Lim

CRC Press
Taylor & Francis Group
Boca Raton London New York

CRC Press is an imprint of the
Taylor & Francis Group, an **informa** business

CRC Press
Taylor & Francis Group
6000 Broken Sound Parkway NW, Suite 300
Boca Raton, FL 33487-2742

International Standard Book Number-13: 978-1-138-90382-1 (Hardback)
International Standard Book Number-13: 978-1-138-54251-8 (Paperback)

**Visit the Taylor & Francis Web site at
http://www.taylorandfrancis.com**

**and the CRC Press Web site at
http://www.crcpress.com**

Printed and bound in the United States of America by Sheridan

To Evan and Tyler,
My Joie de Vivre

To Carole,
My Northern Light

To Wendy,
My Big Sister

To Skip,
My Yoda

Preface

Designing My Life:
Living the Good, the Bad,
and the Ugly

I started this book journey back in November of 2014. For any aspiring author, it's like hitting a jackpot when a reputable publisher picks up your book idea. My type A, overachieving Chinese self said, "I can finish this book in nine months!" Fast-forward to April 2017, and I found I had barely made it to the second draft.

Predictably, life got in the way. Actually, many life-altering events happened. I underwent an upending onslaught of deaths, divorce, loss of wealth, loss of friendships, depression, and almost the loss of the business I had spent the past 15 years building. I had no idea that in the span of six months I actually went through what medical health experts consider to be the top five most stressful life events: death of loved ones; divorce; moving; major illness/injury; and job loss.[1]

Only a handful of people knew about the trauma I was suffering. Everything and anything could trigger and throw me into a depressive mood. One minute I was laughing, and the next I was crying. Work was my only refuge, but even that was hard to manage at times.

I was overwhelmed trying to figure out how to feed my two children and keep their lives as normal as possible, all the while struggling to make payroll for my team. I found myself buried in attorney fees from the divorce, was single-handedly paying my mortgage and maintaining our old home, and keeping up with childcare and tuition. I remember that I was so broke, I actually had to use my kids' piggy bank money to buy groceries. When it came to tapping the piggy bank, I realized I had hit rock bottom. In fact, I had repeated history. I flashed back to how my Dad had to borrow money from my sister and me when he moved out of the house when I was five. So here I was: I had become my father.

I remember attending the Forbes Women's Summit in NYC, where 150 female global leaders and entrepreneurs had assembled to talk and share, and where I found myself sitting across from Moira Forbes. I broke down in tears and revealed that I could barely get out of bed; but there I was, having to "pretend" that I had my shit together in that room filled with "successful" women. What success did I possibly have to share when I had lost my marriage, was perilously close to losing my business because of the divorce, had become a single mother with two boys under the age of 5, and was unsure how or whether to continue my path as a CEO to my team and as an amazing, sharp-witted, sought-after consultant to my clients? The creamy center to all of that candy was that **I was supposed to be writing a book that would teach others how to design their own meaningful lives and brands?** I felt I had become a fraud.

Not surprisingly, it was all too much. I stepped out of the limelight for well over a year. I stopped writing, I stopped hosting workshops, and I stopped speaking. Essentially, I stopped being the Mel Lim I knew.

Then one night, I sat quietly and reflected on how hard I had worked for the last 20 years—averaging 100-hour work weeks since I was 19, and I now had nothing left under my name except for my ability to make money, whatever that means. As soon as I said that out loud, I realized wow—I absolutely have the ability to reinvent myself. I definitely have great earning potential. And I certainly have it within me to make a good life for my children. Then why was I so unhappy? It's not like I hadn't gone through the loss of a loved one or been poor before. I have always lived my life on my own, without rules. I never had a lot to begin with. Both my parents and all of my elders had already passed away. I had experienced three bankruptcies in my lifetime with my family. So this slump of unfortunate events really just constituted another temporary obstacle to overcome.

At that moment, I realized that every trauma, setback, and challenge I had faced in my younger life had all prepared me for this. The nonexistence of safety nets in any form equipped me with the tools and agility I needed to survive and succeed, for myself and for my children. The more I quietly reflected on both my achievements and failures, the more I was drawn to begin making a list of all the tools that I can now share with you today. This book represents my life made manifest, up to this point. It contains all my joys and aspirations, and all of the successes I have brought to my clients. I have used these tools to successfully redesign my life and my career, in less than 20 months.

It is through this "Aha!" moment that I am now able to complete this book, and bring to you my truest self and the hard-won knowledge and wisdom I have gained. I hope you are able to take my humble offering and apply it to your life and work, and live fearlessly, unapologetically, and authentically.

Love,

Mel Lim

Thank You

Carole Jerome, Skip Franklin, Ginger Dhaliwal, Wendy Mills, Megan Lauren, Deborah Hagen, Stephanie Simmons, Angela Blanchard, David Gibson, Heather Stowe, Vanecia Carr, Enrico Cuini, Taryn Rose, Deborah Mills-Scofield, Ellen Petry Leanse, Victor Hsu, Shirinne Alison-Hsu, Debra Chen, Shilpa Shah, Victoria Lakers, Vishal Mehta, Dean Browell, Kriselle Laran, Rod Kosann, Aaron Fulkerson, Karen Krasne, Craig Sewing, Michelle Peranteau, Victoria Tsai, Amanda North, Mari Kuraishi, Bill Eigner, Matt Wozniak, Angela Yeh, Helene Pretsky, Sharon Eucce, Janine Darling, Michael Swartz, Suzanne Ito, Jordan Brady, Sue Hrib, Kenneth Bradshaw, Sook Ling Ong, Li Cheng Chai, Shawn Flint Blair, Julie Jones, Tennyson Pinheiro, Sarah Zaouk, Hazel Ortega, Genevieve Bos, Angela Lee, Bob Upham, Marsha Ann Ralls

Table of Contents

I divided this book into 10 distinct sections that take you on an exploratory journey, asking you to think through your actions and ideas and make thoughtful choices. Each chapter offers a case study or an interview with an amazing person who is changing the world while reconnecting with their dreams, artistic values, and hands-on processes. Every chapter also provides takeaway content that promotes holistic artistry and empowers you to be fully in touch with your whole person, power, and potential.

Table of Contents

You may read the chapters in the order presented, or in the order of your interest. I want you to interact with and experience this work in the way that is most meaningful to you. Ultimately, I ask you to consider your own artisan nature, utilize the resources herein, and connect with a global network of people from all walks of life who mindfully and passionately work to improve the balance of global living.

www.mellim.com

6

Creative Guru 101: Learn to Be Mindful, Accountable, and Trustworthy

Ideation and Creativity

Cultivate the Beginner's Mind

Truth: The Stamp of Authenticity

Imposter Syndrome: Zero Calories in Humble Pie

Accountability: A Measure of Creative Integrity

Fail to Succeed

The Holy Grail of Relationships: Trust

Where Rapid Prototyping Reigns, Trust Wanes

Case Study: Aaron Fulkerson, CEO of MindTouch

Summary: Creative Guru 101

7

Rules of Mastery

The Three Degrees of Motivation: High, Happy, and Passionate

The Hot-Pursuit High

Meaning versus Happiness

Passion versus Passing Fancy

Mel's Motivation Matrix

Rules of Mastery

Case Study: Karen Krasne, CEO of Extraordinary Desserts

Summary: Rules of Mastery

1   *We Are Creative by Nature*

Each of us has been designing our own life and brand since the day we were born. Early on, we may not have had that concept or language to put around this crafting of our individual lives, but essentially that has been our erstwhile endeavor. We are artisanal beings with an inherent nature to create and an instinctive need to belong. We want to be liked, we want to be included, we want to be valued, and we want to hold a certain amount of sway in our personal and professional circles.

We are constantly evolving to a greater, more complete expression of ourselves in the world, and carefully curating what we project, how we appear, and what we want the world in general to know about us. For each of us, our process of becoming can be very different. We may be very deliberate, we may be impulsive, we may be thoughtful and strategic, we may be free-spirited enough to land wherever the wind blows, or we may be happily racing headlong into oblivion, trusting that all will work out in the end.

As a child growing up in Malaysia, I was always very goal-oriented and project-driven. Yes, I was a nerdy, creative type who got excited over bits of colored material and ways to put colors and textures together. I had big visions and not much else. My resources, if I had any, were all internal; yet, I somehow managed to manifest my dreams through focused intention and a lot of hard work. Today those inherent drivers are still very much a part of me, and the intensity with which I feel them has grown exponentially. I always wanted to be a designer and to create products, services and experiences that would be of benefit in the world. Each day I mindfully and actively pursue opportunities to create with integrity and to meticulously craft experiences and products that make the world a better place.

The Whereabouts of Childlike Wonder: Reflect, Redefine, Reinvigorate

Do you remember your childhood: the joy in greeting each new day; that sense of infinite possibility; living in a world without time; and endless role playing as your favorite superhero, where at the end of the day you saved the world?

What were your dreams as a child? How closely have you landed to those dreams in your adult life? Are you still, deep in your soul, that valiant superhero? What do you do in your life every day that you hope has a positive impact on the world now and in the future? How have you set about designing your personal life and brand? What is your process? Do you apply a goal, strategy and flow? Have you explored numerous ways of working and being in the world to see what feels right to you? Or do you meet the world each day as it presents itself and take everything as it comes?

I wrote this book for (closet-superhero) people:

- Frustrated with processes in the workplace that don't allow for failures

- Dealing with clients wanting premium for less

- Trying to build a long-lasting career in a rabbit-race age

- Who understand that there is no fast track to building great brands, products and services

- Caring to develop and craft authentic value through experience and work, and not just "manufactured authority"

- Unwilling to give in to the pressure of social media and technology and trying to bring relevancy and value back by applying their skills in our modern world

- Wanting to thoughtfully create meaningful change in their own lives and the lives of others through their work

- Hoping to nurture a team, and build a company culture that is inspiring and authentic

- Inspired by their love for craft and reiterative processes that foster accountability and focus, nurture discovery, and help us think, play and do

- Who just want to mindfully evolve and grow creatively

How the Leopard Got Its Spots

I crafted this book as an exercise in mindful creating.
It looks at some of the gifts and challenges presented
by technology while we strive to impact our world
in meaningful ways. One of the things that struck
me early on in my design career was the velocity at
which everything moves globally. Our instant-access
information age can cause us to perceive life as a
frenetic rabbit race.

That has only gotten more pronounced as technology evolves. I
often feel like a turtle, wanting to slow things down and move at a
thoughtful pace in order to ensure balance and impart mindfulness
and craftsmanship into my work. While this may be difficult, I believe
it is both possible and necessary. This book offers a strategy for living
mindfully as artisanal beings who wittingly shape the future. I hope
you will find it to be a useful and aspirational metric and guide for
reframing your thinking whenever you approach a project
or challenge.

Do you want your work/designs/life to impart uniqueness, value, and thoughtful creation?

Are you motivated by excellence?

Is integrity an essential component of your "bottom line"?

Do you proudly take ownership and remain accountable for what you create?

If you've answered "yes" to two or more of these questions, you may be a Turtle at heart.

What do I mean? Well, your perception of and approach to time can distinguish you as a craftsman, a rule breaker, and a true ARTISAN committed to inspiring meaningful change in the world.

What's in a Turtle?
Symbology for Our Time

Across time and cultures, turtles have inspired our curiosity, our compassion, our comic sensibility, and our connection to our earth. In his book *Animal Speak*, author Ted Andrews discusses these most ancient of vertebrate animals from a biological, spiritual/symbolic, and practical teaching perspective.[2] For example, turtles have amazing survival skills and strategies. They hear and smell well, and can distinguish colors. These dinosaur-like creatures have a slow metabolism and serve as a strong reminder of how important it is to live at the pace of one's own natural flow.

This is a creature in touch with the seasons, that possesses an intuitive relationship with time. It hibernates in winter, betraying an inherent awareness that all things happen in their own time, and that sometimes going dormant is necessary and good. In its roundness and literal grounded essence, the turtle represents holistic balance, self-containment and connection to the earth. It summons its resources from deep within itself as it plods deliberately through life wearing its home on its back. To move impulsively, without care or awareness of its surroundings, can result in imbalance or becoming upended. The wise-faced turtle serves as a totem for mindful calculation, thoughtful action, and balance.

My Artisan Awakening: Experience, Observation, Transcendence

My own artisan awakening and careful attention to craft, detail, and the refinement of processes were inspired by my life experiences, from my earliest recollections to present time. It began when I was five years old.

My late father, who had suffered bankruptcy and business failure, left our family. This turned my mother into a workaholic. She was a traditional Chinese woman and had not only my sister and me to support, but also her nine other siblings and our grandparents. I learned early on that business IS personal.

> I learned early on that business IS personal.

My parents never sheltered us from the real-world problems they faced. At some level, I think they were the most transparent parents. They would tell us the truth about money and life, and they modeled hard work, perseverance, and success. But perhaps the greatest gift they gave me was the encouragement to dream, to visualize, to pursue happiness, and to believe that success is possible, whatever your circumstances.

I watched my mother raise herself from the ranks of a salesperson, to a supervisor, then a manager and ultimately the CEO of her own interior design and furniture manufacturing company. And my father ultimately rebuilt his business into a multi-million-dollar powerhouse developing land, hotels, and shopping centers. The hardships I experienced early in life fueled my hunger to create and ensured my discipline and drive. Always alert to my environment and opportunities, efficient processes and successful methodologies, I am especially attentive to every detail when I take on projects as CEO of my design firm, *Mel Lim* and President of my startup consultancy *Maspira Groupe.*

As a woman committed to her craft, I am equally committed to working with people who understand passion for detail and who value artisan processes. I seek out good clients. I don't mean clients who are easy to work with, who pay on time, who have the potential for being ongoing sources of great projects, and who think that every idea I throw their way is an optimal solution. While that may contribute to a "perfect marriage" between this design artisan and her clients, I am instead referring to clients and others who really appreciate all the effort that goes into every single pencil stroke or pixel I create and who care about their own craft. This is challenging, but there are those who share my values/manifesto: constantly strive to better one's craft; relearn and refine tools and processes; create products, services, art, music, literature etc. that inspire others; and help improve lives. I want to serve and spend time with people who are connected to their inner artisan, who want to make a positive impact on the world, and who have the creative heart, passion and balanced conviction of that metaphorical "Turtle."

Mindful processes and the desire to do better for oneself and others distinguishes the awakened artisan. As a "group," we are often hiding in plain sight. We tend to be introverted creatives cocooned in silos, producing our art, pouring our souls into our reiterative artisanal processes. As a collective, we could learn so much from one another, and perhaps not feel so alone and isolated in striving to deliver maximum quality work at the speed of excellence. I am not an apologist when it comes to taking the time to explore optimal solutions. Even though we live in a fast-paced world, I believe that by waking up to our own natures and honoring our processes and methodologies, this mindful passion for our work can be our differentiator and not our demise.

I am proud to be someone who takes time to create, who prizes the exceptional over the expedient, who knows that the shortest distance between problem and solution is not necessarily a straight line, and who values long-term, mutually productive relationships.

With this book, I would like to help others who care to explore or refine their inner artisan to discover those processes and methodologies that best support their creative spark, and to find belonging and camaraderie in a creative collective of like-minded talent committed to quality and craftsmanship in all that they do. Let's start a movement. What reassurance there is in realizing that mindful creating and craftsmanship are neither anomaly or archaic. We are many, and we are having the time of our life taking the time to create.

Aesop for Our Time

Fables represent snapshots of human and societal conditions. Aesop's fable *The Tortoise and the Hare* offers a loose framework with which to examine the world in which we now find ourselves.[3] As you may recall, the tortoise and hare enter into a race which the hare might easily have won, except that he took a nap along the way thinking the tortoise would never catch up, and finished last.

In today's world, we rush, like the hare, headlong toward some arbitrary finish line. And in our rushing, the nap we take along the way is a nap of deliberate forgetfulness. We forget to take time to appreciate beauty around us. We forget how to listen and how to connect deeply. We forget the value of quality and crafted detail. We forget how to explore, discover and think for ourselves. We forget how to breathe.

I have noticed that as technology and social media infiltrate every aspect of our lives, we seem to be trying to live at the speed of digital. The urgency to outdo, outperform, and outpace one another feels pressurizing, polarizing and even isolating. We obsess over our popularity; i.e., the number of fans we have on Twitter; the number of likes we receive on Facebook; the quantity of connections we have on LinkedIn. In this mad-dash existence that puts our adrenals into overdrive, I find myself pondering some important questions:

• Are we amputating our senses as technology becomes our eyes, ears, hands, legs, and even our brain?

- Are we stunting our curiosity by forgetting how to discover and explore for ourselves? Do we still know how to try and fail gracefully, own our mistakes, and remain accountable for our actions/decisions?

- Are we in touch with our real motivations, drivers, and definitions of success?

- Do we have the skills to connect, listen, understand and problem-solve effectively?

- Has our "instant gratification" mindset permeated our creative processes?

- Are true craft and creativity extinct?

- Is life an immersion in the superficial?

When I consider the impact of our technology and velocity of life on how we create the experiences we enjoy, and on our experience of life itself, I feel justified in registering some alarm. Adapting to things superficial, and accepting mediocrity is not an optimum way of life. I would like to think that a collective of creative people focused on rediscovering the art of true craft can restore the depth and integrity of how we create meaningful experiences. Such a movement has the potential to create a social enterprise, a collaborative economy. If we are all committed to living our lives as high art, we can model inspiration and motivate each other's daily engagements, all the while building communities, businesses, and a better world together.

> Are we amputating our senses as technology becomes our eyes, ears, hands, legs, and even our brains?

An Artisan's Oath

What matters to each one of us as individuals may not be important to others. We know that. We all have our personal missions, family and cultural backgrounds, ambitions, etc., that shape our ability to define our time and how we spend it. But I believe that each of us has the responsibility and ability to create the best life possible.

When we are living an authentic and fulfilling life, the world around us benefits simply from the joy we emanate. I also feel that designers, brand managers, CMOs, VPs, and others involved in creating products and services that affect the lives of others, whoever they may be and wherever they may live, have a huge responsibility to deliver a premiere experience.

The creative spirit and design matter. They matter because they do not exist in a bubble. Artists have always had the luxury of creating their pieces for their own purpose, interpretation, and experience and later (almost as an afterthought) to be enjoyed by many. For example, Leonardo da Vinci's obsession with *sfumato,* a technique creating transitions between light and shade that are imperceptible to the human eye, gave us the Mona Lisa to ponder and admire while it gave da Vinci a deeper knowledge of how his scientific observations could be applied in portraiture. But the rest of us? Well, designers, for instance, may be filled with inspiration, but our motivation is problem solving through the creation and execution of optimal experiences with which people interact.

Beginning at the inception of each idea, we look at the experiences we care to create through the eyes of the beholder, the customer. We examine the intricacies of every single layer and interaction, from the moment a customer or user is made aware of a company and a brand. Artisan designers make the effort, every step of the way, to craft touch points and make them memorable. If any one of us does not take the time to explore ideas and solutions, or to tell the deeper truths in what we create, we are not being authentic, we are not delivering on what we promise. The promise we make when we first decide to become a creative person is that we will do our work with passion, love and greatest integrity.

Let's all take a moment to reflect. Listen to the voice of your conscience and challenge yourself from within. Ask yourself honestly what you have done lately to improve your own and other people's lives. Do you care whether or not what you do positively impacts the world? What have you done to improve your own skillset so that you can better serve others? Are you ready to master your own life and craft, realizing that by doing so you will possibly instill value and aspiration into future generations? Do you have the tenacity and patience of a true artisan?

In the pages that follow, we will investigate how and what we lose when we choose automation over artisanship, quantity over quality, and expediency over mindfulness. As an antidote, we will explore strategies to help people reframe their approach to value creation:

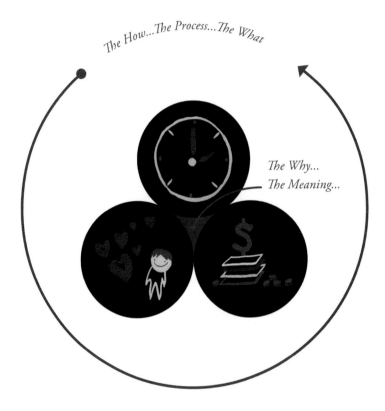

Value Creation

With storytelling as our medium, we will showcase examples of real-world "turtles," and present interviews and case studies of businesses and artisans taking the time to master their craft and make a difference. In the expediency of this Rabbit Age in which we live, we will call on all readers to embrace and embody the wisdom of becoming The Turtle.

The Five Indicators of Turtle Tenacity

"Turtles" share a number of important, inherent, and persistent qualities that sometimes make it difficult for them to fit into this world of 30-second trends and perpetually immature design executions. See if these key indicators apply to you:

Perseverance

You care deeply to be able to take the time to work with care and deliberation.

Self-sufficiency

You actively seek out opportunities to refine your skills and heighten your sensibilities.

Connectivity

You understand the connection between and to all things and recognize that your work and how you arrive at it impacts the balance of global living.

Accountability

You feel deeply that your work is an extension of you. Just as turtles cannot separate from their shells, neither can artisans be separate from their work.

Longevity

You care to create original and quality work that will last beyond the immediate, will serve as the foundation and building blocks for subsequent great ideas, and will offer visible proof of the integrity of work well-crafted and a job well done.

A Vetting Process: People and Brands Selection Criteria

It was important to select people and brands that reflected qualities specific to the message and metric for success being communicated in this book. Together, the criterion create a framework and a roadmap for people to use as they reexamine their approach to designing their life and brand. Think of each criterion as a tool you use in conjunction with what you have and who you are so that the success you realize feels personal, meaningful and deeply satisfying. The criteria I applied to selecting those presented in each case study and that I offer you include the following touchstones and measuring principles:

Vision

Possessing vision implies having some sense of where you are going and how you prefer to end up. Vision can seem nebulous and etheric, but when pondered and richly imagined, thoughts do manifest.We have only to look around our world and see that everything that exists once began as a single thought and someone's vision of what could be. Vision is often aspirational, and aside from having a view toward some financial success or acknowledgment and reward, it can also incorporate a desire to elevate society and culture, improve environments, and help civilization evolve positively.

Noble Values

Our values are our behavior guidelines. They direct how we move through life and inform our integrity. They help dictate not only how we interact with and impact the world around us, but often how we will end up feeling about ourselves at the end of the day. Our ability to adhere to and craft our world according to our values can mean the difference between niggling dissatisfaction and a life well lived. The people and brands chosen for this exploration into designing one's life reflected some or all of the following noble values:

- The desire to create a product or service through mastery of a craft

- Uncompromising dedication to quality

- A desire to have social and/or environmental impact

- A commitment to doing what is right over what is easy

- A diligent focus on crafting memorable, meaningful experiences

- A desire for longevity of life, brand, and influence

- An intention towards enrichment of people's lives, memories, artistic appreciation, the environment, the future of science, etc.

Curiosity/Initiative

This book showcases persons or brands that are innately curious about exploring, discovering, and learning new tools for improving their own or other people's lives. Such people or brands are not driven by peer pressure or market trends. Rather, they are self-starting individuals motivated by their intrinsic drive to grow. Often they have conducted a full assessment and have active use of their skills sets.

Grit

Adversity nurtures growth and evolution. Challenges and obstacles test perseverance, passion, and commitment, and often reveal opportunities. Grit is a trait of authenticity that permits pausing and regrouping for an emboldened reach toward success. People with grit are not put off or stopped by challenges and obstacles. Instead, they instinctively dig deep within themselves, sharpen their focus, and manifest success through adherence to their vision. Grit is code for "unstoppable."

Focused Commitment/Dedication

Often, people find many things about which to be passionate. New things peak interest and curiosity. But real commitment extends beyond infatuation with the new. It is as much about knowing oneself completely and deeply as it is about adhering to a vision, values, and the hope for success.

Time Management

Time factors and multiple commitments can also insinuate themselves as challenges to producing our best within a limited time frame. Flow is essential. How you build, prioritize, set firm boundaries, filter out the extraneous, and master your day tremendously impact your ability to move beyond progress to realized success.

Summary: We Are Creative by Nature

This book is an exercise in mindful creating in a high-velocity world with its ever-evolving technology. It offers a strategy for wittingly shaping the future and inspiring meaningful change through our craft and artisanship. Within these pages I employ the metaphor of the turtle to describe a movement toward slowing things to a thoughtful pace where integrity and accountability inform our process and the fruits of our efforts are imbued with uniqueness, value, and craftsmanship.

As an ancient symbol of holistic balance, self-reliance, grounded essence and connection to the earth, the turtle provides an apt metaphor for the importance of living at the pace of one's natural flow. Moving deliberately and carefully, it serves as a totem for mindful calculation and thoughtful action. For the purposes of this book, the turtle invites commitment to craft and attentiveness to detail in the real-world environments where creativity competes with efficiency.

My parents were business people and CEOs of their own companies who never sheltered our family from the hard truths about work, perseverance, money, life, success and failure. Their work ethic and passion for artisan processes have informed my own approach to my business and craft. Through their example I have learned how to source great clients who care about the crafted effort that goes into their projects.

Creatives who identify with the turtle are often hiding in plain sight, feeling alone and isolated in prizing the exceptional over the expedient. I would like to reassure you closet artisans that mindful creating and craftsmanship are neither anomaly or archaic. You are not alone. We should start a movement, a collective of like-minded talent committed to quality and craftsmanship. I would like us to remember how to explore, discover, create, think for ourselves, and breathe.

The speed and urgency of our digital lives prompts some important questions:

- Has technology replaced our eyes, ears, hands, legs, and brain?

- Have we forgotten how to discover, explore, try, fail, own our mistakes, and be accountable?

- Are we in touch with our motivations?

- Can we listen and problem-solve effectively?

- Has our "instant gratification" mindset permeated our creative processes?

- Are craft, creativity, and authenticity extinct?

The creative spirit matters. Each of us has the responsibility to deliver premiere experiences and positively impact the world. When we master our own life and craft, we can help instill value and aspiration into future generations. We must discern if we have the tenacity, skill set, and patience to be true artisans:

- Do we work with care and deliberation?

- Do we actively seek opportunities to refine our skills?

- Is our work an extension of ourselves?

- Do we create original, quality work that has longevity?

"Beauty can get people to try a product or service and the inherent product value keeps the customers coming back. "

—Victor Hsu, CEO of Axure

2   *Fast or Fastidious*

What's the Rush?

Would you marry someone with whom you just shared a 30-second speed date? Would you let someone who speed-read a book on cardiology perform open-heart surgery on you? If you dined out at an expensive restaurant, would you be satisfied with a microwaved entrée? When it comes to the products and services that we typically signify as having value, prestige, and even longevity, one single element factors into their creation: time. So why is it that life, creativity and design processes, from ideation to development to implementation, are all happening on the fast track? What might the implications be?

At today's speed of life, culture is instant coffee. In our "on-demand" world, a fast turnaround of ideas feeds our increasing need for immediate gratification. New problems and challenges demand instantaneous solutions. The market is hot, competition is steep, and the yen for trend and all that will satiate it are as close as our nearest fingertip technology. Or so we think. The urgency to compete drives this reckless "need for speed." And in this frenzy, we are moving toward a heightened state of impermanence: All we hold true in this moment will be obsolete in the next. And the creative solutions and designs that seem valid in this instant have no value or application in the next. Our "I want it and I want it now" mindset has permeated our lives, our creative outlook and our design processes. We must slow things down, simmer our thoughts, steep our strategies, and craft our ideas into existence. It takes time to do something exceptional.

It feels as if we live in a time with no time for time. Our culture, our global economy, our instant information era reflect an increasing need for speed. We demand the expeditious and efficient delivery of goods and services, and our focus on the fast track gives a whole new meaning to the term "the Human Race." And yet our relationship to time seems paradoxical because we assign value and prestige to products and services that take time to create.

> Time IS the new currency, and as such, we really need to establish our relationship with it and redefine it ourselves.

Time IS the new currency, and as such, we really need to establish our relationship with it and redefine it for ourselves. How many times a day do you say to yourself, or say out loud to someone else, "I'm too busy to _you fill in the blank._" Perhaps you are too busy to jog, do yoga, dine out with pals, walk the dog, listen to a friend's problems, visit a relative, or even take vacation. We live in a world where being busy defines and indicates success. But you must remember, a creative's toolbox is only as good as his or her experience. Balance is the key to enriching experiences. And enriching experiences inform all aspects, including the professional side, of life.

Throughout our day, everything seems to come at us at once. Everyone wants everything NOW—family, significant others, friends, collaborators, team members, clients, their customers. And you expect the same of others. How do you manage all of it without burning out with a fizzle and pop? The answer? Take a ZEN moment. Refrain from checking your Facebook page or typing a tweet.

Setting Mindful Intentions

Devote a few mindful minutes out of your life at the beginning of every day to validate your life and purpose and to ask yourself some important questions:

Validation

I am grateful for this precious life I have been gifted. I will not waste it. I will use my energies to grow in knowledge, improve myself, benefit others, and make the world a better place.

What do I want to accomplish this day and why am I doing it?
Will I learn from it and love doing it?
Will it be a good use of my time?
Will I need to do something differently?
Who will benefit and who will be empowered?

Answering these questions helps you set your intentions for the hours that follow. Every day before stepping out into my studio, I mindfully ask myself these questions. This practice helps me prioritize, and as a CEO, it helps me delegate. Am I spearheading projects today, overseeing work, marketing the business, pursuing client acquisition, managing human resources, or any of the myriad and challenging tasks that comes from being owner, CEO, and CCO of an innovation strategy firm? If someone else is better suited to perform the tasks, I delegate to them. I delegate not because I am lazy, but because I work in a high-performance team environment. I work in an ecosystem where expectations are high, from clients, to their customers, and right on down to my team members' needs. I manage personalities and expectations. I make sure my team is happy and performs at their best.

Recalibrating time by taking that ZEN moment to set intentions helps me filter through a complex chain of issues and decisions required from me. I can prioritize them, and I can ask myself why and how do I need to do things differently. It helps me discern what does and does not work. And I am also conscious of what I am choosing NOT to do that day. Every day is a quest for time and efficiency so that I can shift the majority of my focus onto things that matter. In this way, I end up gaining time because my actions are driven by my intentions, and I am not spinning in circles trying to attend to every little thing. With the WHAT and WHY taken care of, I can focus on the HOW.

As a designer, I like to WOW my clients. With each new project, I desire to create something exceptional. But in our "I want it now!!" era with technology tools that expedite execution and design processes, from ideation to development, I wonder if creatives are pressed to settle for merely "acceptable" solutions that lack any real craft, quality or hope of longevity? Is our fast pace making us both masters and consumers of mediocrity?

As the world hurls willy nilly toward some inconceivable destiny, I ponder the seeming lack of understanding about what creativity requires. Our accelerated living has created unrealistic expectations around the creative process, along with a world of products possessing questionable quality and very short shelf life. Creatives need time to innovate and create, and they need to build in time for failed attempts. Failure happens, even under the most arduous, deliberate and painstaking of innovation and execution processes. Yet, by spending time thoroughly exploring viable options, failure can be mitigated or minimized. You can't rush excellence. Let's not forget the old adage "Haste Makes Waste."

Creativity is a free spirit. It likes to breathe, flutter, dance, dive, dote, and dally, and it thrives on sensory interaction. Immersion into the material "is-ness" of life is the clay and the kiln of creativity. Playing with light, shadow, form, physics, and toys that are tools for new ways of seeing all contribute to inspired innovating. Engaging in puppetry, LEGOs construction, photography, tinker toys, watercolor, etc., all are the ickey, stickey, gooey sweetness of exploration and discovery that leads to great new ideas, products, and services that can benefit people, societies, and the environment in which we live.

Creative discovery does not necessarily happen within a tight time frame. Limiting the playground of imagination to the use of technical tools and solutions within a time-poor pressure cooker represses and subverts creativity. The creative processes and play that lead to good ideas can get spun out with the bathwater by the centrifugal force of rapid idea generation and prototyping. Pace affects thought, process, product and even personal relationships and well-being.

The acceleration of life, and our distance from all we once considered germane to the "creative process" has deprived us of the sweetness of hands-on creating and the finer details we associate with it. No longer do young people have a sense of the "discovery process." Art and its processes seem lost. Now people paint, draw, and draft on screens. Photographers' life works are digital and stored on hard drives. No longer do we flip through albums. With fingertip technology, children do not need to visit libraries, page through the stacks, explore, and sift through tangible articles. And relationships are begun and ended in text messages and Skype conversations. Building relationships with others face to face is old fashioned and inconvenient. While we may have gained the whole world with our internet and information age, is it possible that we have literally lost "touch" with everything?

How can we disrupt this overwhelming trend and reclaim the time necessary to enjoy the sensory connections that inform our artisanal insights and our lives in general?

How can we be more mindful of time and not allow our creative process to be rushed so we can mindfully create?

What would the turtle do?

A Lesson in Time

Creativity takes time. The assignment of restrictive and immediate deadlines limits the cultivation of original and well-thought-out ideas.

In 2011, a Hungarian ad agency—Café Creative—sought to demonstrate that the fullness of creativity directly correlates to the amount of time allowed to complete a project.[4] The agency visited a classroom and asked the school children to complete the drawing of a clock. In the first exercise, the children were given 10 seconds in which to complete the project. In the second exercise, they were given 10 minutes to perform the same task. The results were documented in a video entitled *Deadlines*. After 10 seconds, the children's drawings allowed only rudimentary development of an initial idea. But with 10 minutes to create, the clock drawings showed imagination and original thought, with the clock face integrated into other faces and backgrounds to enrich meaning and even tell a story.

Time is the incubator of creative thinking. While some people may assert that they are "grace under pressure" and do their best work when they are in a time crunch, research actually proves the opposite is true, and that great ideas take time. In a multi-year research program investigating time pressure and creativity, Harvard Business School professor Teresa Amabile discovered that overall, very high levels of time pressure should be avoided if you want to foster creativity on a consistent basis.[5] However, if a tight deadline is absolutely unavoidable, managers can try to preserve creativity by protecting people from distractions and work fragmentation. In fact, even what most would consider prime motivators such as money and fame actually caused a decrease in creativity as opposed to when people are motivated primarily by the interest, enjoyment, satisfaction and challenge of the work itself. Amabile also found that behaviors such as procrastination hindered performance on projects requiring creative thinking.

Good ideas cannot be rushed. Creativity involves discovering, exploring and organizing those ideas. Ranking ideas from most to least viable or compatible, and then shaping them into form and function can help to further flush out additional ideas. Epiphanies and sudden insights are the exception and not the norm. In a January, 2006 *TIME* magazine article, "The Hidden Secrets of the Creative Mind," Washington University psychologist R. Keith Sawyer suggested that taking time off from working on a problem can activate different areas of the brain that can help us see relationships, lead to new insights and actually help us unlock new ideas.[6] In creativity research, he refers to the three B's—Bathtub, Bed, and Bus—as places where ideas are known to suddenly emerge. Ideas always build on what came before, so collaboration, research, and analogies can help spark new insights. The key is to have the time to innovate, and then work hard at it.

What else gets sacrificed when we don't take the time to evaluate environments or think ideas through? If the discovery process can be done hastily, who needs research, right? And if design can be done rapidly, then logically the final production can be done in the same manner. What then do you think we are grooming the client to expect in terms of quality? The temptation exists to promote an acceptance of mediocrity. The argument becomes "If the users are happy with the rough prototype, why does a company need to spend more time and money beautifying it. Just ship it!"

Whoa! Not so fast. The true artisan will have that niggling feeling of having delivered an unfinished work, of not having created to completion and perfection.

> When you're a carpenter making a beautiful chest of drawers, you're not going to use a piece of plywood on the back, even though it faces the wall and nobody will see it.
>
> —Steve Jobs

Consider what Steve Jobs once said:

When you're a carpenter making a beautiful chest of drawers, you're not going to use a piece of plywood on the back, even though it faces the wall and nobody will see it. You'll know it's there so you're going to use a beautiful piece of wood on the back. For you to sleep well at night, the aesthetic, the quality, has to be carried all the way through.

As artisans, we must insist on the resources necessary for crafting our work. We know instinctively when we have left something unexplored and unfinished, and it grates at our creative integrity. We alone are responsible for maintaining the integrity of our craft. We must take a stand. If the turtle does not stick out its neck, it does not move forward in any direction or begin to ingest the vital nutrients necessary for preserving life.

A Time and a Place for Prototyping

Ideation is that stage in the creative process where new ideas are generated, further developed and communicated. It is the point where customer and end-user requirements are listened to, understood, and interpreted. And it is the moment where opportunities are identified for innovation.

Time is spent in ideation brainstorming a diversity of ideas to arrive at quality solutions. Rapid prototyping's rightful place rests within this cycle that spans the gamut of innovation, development, and actualization. It can be used to test competing ideas or concepts selected for their ability to meet a critical criterion of requirements, and to therefore help identify the strongest ideas delivering the best quality and value.

Typically, good and successful design is arrived at through discovery. The process is non-linear, vague, scattered, and may be counterintuitive or paradoxical. Ideas can be born through accident or acumen. For example, an ex-director at P&G hired a team of designers (not brand strategists) to see where the company might go next in its product lines. The designers created mood boards and stumbled across a pattern that revealed that millennials don't like doing laundry and love for their clothes to look broken in and distressed. Previous brand strategists had been designing for Moms. But at the end of the day, after taking time to meander around and gain real insights into consumer lifestyles, the designers successfully reframed "wicked problems," developed innovative solutions, and tapped into new markets for the global brand.[7]

Get Your Hands Dirty

We must reclaim our power and function, and rediscover process. Process is like going to a tearoom for tea and enjoying all of the sensuousness and ceremony that surround selecting, steeping, pouring, and drinking tea. People will pay premium for process and want to support those who are taking time to do things well. A market for hands-on artisanship and craft exists. People long for it. It's time to stop sacrificing quality for competitiveness.

It's time to get back to basics, back to old-school principles, and to doing the unexpected. Yes, it can be hard. It can be challenging. But the most rewarding work is the work that challenges us, forces us to reach beyond our known limits, and to evolve to that next level of accomplishment and excellence.

What is the value in doing something by hand? In flowing hands-on processes into our creative discovery and craft? Touching something gives us an automatic relationship to it. Immersion in the physical reality of something deepens our own knowledge and awareness of it, broadens our definition of it, allows us to make connections, enables us to see it in new ways, and enriches our overall experience. We have the opportunity to tangibly assess usability, discern new needs, integrate new functions or features, and maybe recalibrate design priorities. Moray Callum, Design Director of Ford Motor's North American Brands, had this to say about interacting with something in the physical world versus the digital world:

> Driving a vehicle is a personal thing; you want it to feel safe and trustworthy, but also like a companion you wouldn't mind spending a very intimate 30 minutes with every day to and from work. And while a computer-generated rendering might be precise, a computer model won't tell you what it's like to actually experience a car's design, standing next to it. People still buy real cars. They don't buy digital cars.[8]

When we touch something in the process of our creating it, we have a very real sense of what it took to "make" it, of the effort behind it. We get a cellular and muscle memory of the creative process, which deepens our own appreciation of it, and makes it memorable and valuable.

Five, Six, Seven, Eight, What Do We Appreciate?

I remember years ago when my late father made my ex-husband finish all of the food on his plate. My father admonished us saying, "You young people just don't know what it takes to grow a grain of rice ..."

Embarrassed, I quickly turned to my ex and said, "Ignore my father. He is an old Chinese man." Fast forward 15 years later, and I found myself preaching to my clients and my team saying, "How do you have appreciation for something, if you don't know the history and process behind it? Not everything can and should be automated, even the process of making a grain of rice. There are people in China who wake up at 4:00 in the morning to plough and tend the rice paddies, while we are busy flushing the rice we didn't consume down the garbage disposal." The lessons of my father had indeed taken root and were beginning to bear fruit. I found myself insisting on an appreciation of "the process" and the time involved in cultivating what we create, and appreciation for what it takes to bring our work to the table.

Deciding who we are as professionals, what we hope to create in the world, how we care to relate to our clients, and knowing our abilities, values and work ethics are our first steps to setting priorities as creatives and artisans. We must review our understanding and relationship to "process." It is time to rediscover listening, waiting, observing, experimenting, and reviewing for relevancy. It is time to employ our bare hands—draw, design, and doodle—and find out if we still have expertise in hands-on processes should technology ever go dark someday.

We must not equate our relevancy with the screens that we touch each day. It is important to remember that technology is a tool. It is there to assist us in our work, but it is not the work itself. Everything that we expect technology to do for us expeditiously, we must also be able to replicate manually. Otherwise, the creative/artist is not the person but rather the technology. It is not the creative's brain that is constantly being developed, rewired, and enhanced but rather it is the technology hardware and software that are being re-versioned, next-generationed, rolled out, and obsolesced almost in the same breath.

To design for brands, we must first design for people.

To design for people, we must first understand culture.

To understand culture we must first understand history.

To understand history, we must first respect traditions.

And to do all of the above, we must give it time.

Time to fully absorb, experience, feel, nurture, taste,

see…where all of our senses are challenged and provoked.

That is design.

That is art.

That is what it takes to design and create for people, for

brands, and for a better world.

That is what it means to be a gloriously grounded "turtle."

Case Study: Victoria Tsai, CEO of Tatcha

Tatcha embodies what we call the Turtle Master. As a business devoted to Japanese beauty, Tatcha has successfully proven that a startup CAN in fact grow and scale without sacrificing its core values, great products and customer experience. Founder Victoria Tsai graduated with an MBA from Harvard, married, had a daughter, and founded Tatcha. The first round of funding for her entrepreneurial venture included selling her engagement ring, furniture and car. And she started Tatcha when she was pregnant.

Different business models and different desired exits require different financing strategies. Victoria hopes to create a company and a brand that will be around for a hundred years, so it's important that her financing strategy matches that goal. For years, her company was largely boot-strapped. As she says, when you put your money and your family's money in the company, you don't play fast and loose with cash.

In creating the business, Victoria feels she has gained a 75-person family and the opportunity to do work that she loves with people she admires. She looks forward to seeing the company and her teammates realize their amazing potential and truly cannot think of anything she has lost or that she regrets.

Giving hope to aspiring entrepreneurs and mompreneurs, Victoria insists that entrepreneurship can happen at any time in your life or career. While it might seem like many startups these days are helmed by a 21-year-old developer, one of the most successful entrepreneurs she knows didn't get his start until he was 50.

Being an entrepreneur requires complete and total commitment; if you're dedicated, you can start a company at any age or with any family situation. Victoria's mom was an entrepreneur with two children, and a new immigrant to this country without a safety net. In watching her, Victoria learned that being a mother and an entrepreneur could be done and requires the focused commitment similar to any working mom. She also likens entrepreneurship to pregnancy: you can't be half-pregnant and you can't be half an entrepreneur.

A recent article in Forbes suggested that even after graduating with an MBA from Harvard, getting married, having a daughter, and founding Tatcha, Victoria's mother was "not impressed," and it was not until she was on QVC that her mother was truly proud. Victoria downplays her mother's cool reaction to her success insisting that it wasn't so much that her mom wasn't impressed. It was more that when you assume that somebody is capable of anything, it's less earth shattering when they accomplish it.

And accomplish she has, implementing artisanship in her approach to value creation, time and money. Tatcha has realized a 10,000% growth rate without VC funding and delivers only the best and highest-quality products (which can be seen through its ingredients, product packaging, product delivery, and customer service). Victoria suggested that for a "regular" business, it would not make sense to create handwritten notes or custom packaging design. But for Tatcha, those elements are all part of the brand promise, as she delivers rich history, culture and traditions from Japan to the customer's doorstep.

Tatcha embraces five core values, each inspired by the founder's Japanese heritage:

Shojin

Dedication to excellence; striving every day to do something better. Tatcha applies this in everything it does, from its efficacious and beautiful formulas and carefully-designed packaging to its world-class customer service. The Tatcha company culture believes they can come to work tomorrow and do even better than the day before.

Seiren

Integrity and humility, drawn from Bushido principles of beauty and enlightenment in simplicity. Tatcha may be a quickly growing company, but they care to maintain the startup mentality and the feeling of being a family. Additionally, customer service isn't just about products and the bottom line—it's about truly serving the customers, and making sure every part of their journey with Tatcha is a joy. There's no ego on the team.

Yuki

Having the courage to challenge convention and push boundaries in order to benefit others. Tatcha has the opportunity to do things differently than the rest of the industry and needs to embrace it. Yuki also means taking chances, like the company's Room to Read partnership, because it is the right thing to do.

Kizuna

A deep human connection that transcends time and space. Tatcha strives to ensure that everything its customers see, whether it's the website or the newest formula, will spark joy for them. The reason they write notes and put so much emphasis on the Customer Love team is because they always want customers to know they can speak to a real person at Tatcha, which creates a genuine connection.

Makoto

Authenticity; a deep sense of being genuine and true. It is crucial to the Tatcha culture that they practice simplicity and authenticity in everything they do.

Victoria offers that there are areas of business where you certainly should be lean, efficient and fast. For example, they always require efficient decision making and communication within the organization and empower people to make decisions at multiple levels to avoid bottlenecks.

On the other hand, there are other areas where there is no substitute for meticulous work. When it comes to the formulas, design and customer service, they always take their time because that's the only way to do it right. If they're talking to a customer, they never want the customer to feel as if they're being rushed off the phone. Tatcha will never launch a formula that's anything less than best in class, even if it takes four years and a hundred tries (as its SPF did). Tatcha is deeply committed to creating a collection worthy of its clients, and that process takes time.

Victoria hopes that the efforts Tatcha has taken to deliver a sense of history, culture and traditions comes across in everything they do, from the rituals they re-create to the ingredients they use, their formulary philosophy, their customer service, their partnership with Room to Read, and their transparency as a company. The best way to scale these extraordinary practices is through the people they hire. The best way to grow a company is letting people do work they take pride in, and giving them company values in which they believe. When the Tatcha team speaks with customers, retailers and press, they aren't reciting a message. They speak from their heart about their brand.

Victoria is building her business for the long haul and not for the quick bottom line. She has an impeccable ability to stay focused and identify key signals amidst distracting noise. In her opinion, trends are noise. She doesn't study or watch competitors, as getting caught up in beauty trends will only water down what Tatcha is working to create. She also sees a trend around startups, where entrepreneurs are focused on raising a lot of money and making a quick exit. There are very few independent beauty brands left at a meaningful size. You hear a lot of buzz about these successful companies, but the quick exit isn't Tatcha's goal.

Tatcha's customers are a signal. They keep the company on track and say what they need. Tatcha has also built a team that acts as a signal. Victoria genuinely appreciates when someone challenges an idea or a decision because they feel it doesn't align with the company's value system.

In order to stay focused, Victoria always starts with the objective. She begins every call or meeting with the phrase, "The purpose of this meeting is…" She makes sure to be crystal-clear about the mission of the company, what it owes each of its stakeholders, and what it must deliver to make good on those promises. That way she knows what she must do each day to make that happen.

For her business, Victoria travels back and forth to Japan from the Bay Area, and spends time with Japanese scientists, researchers, and modern geishas. The most important thing she has learned in working with different cultures is to listen much more than you speak. She feels that as an entrepreneur, you don't have much in the way of resources, leverage or proof that you are worth someone's time or effort. In order to convince someone that your goals are aligned and that you'll make great partners, you must first listen to understand how they see the world. That's particularly true with people from other cultures, but it's a good rule of thumb overall.

Victoria is a self-described "sushi connoisseur in chief." She feels that at a very basic level, sushi is her default food. It's hard to find time to exercise and eat healthy when you have a young child and a company, and are often on the road. Sushi has become her go-to meal choice. It also reminds her that there is true elegance in simplicity. Sushi is just raw fish, rice and seaweed; and yet, with mastery, it can be turned into the world's finest cuisine. Sure, it's easy to smash a bunch of food items together, but true, artfully crafted simplicity takes time and effort and is well worth the wait.

Questions to Ask Yourself When Designing Experiences

1. What are your core values and aspirations?

2. Do your experiences and connections matter?

3. Do you believe that you are designing individual, social, and cultural experiences with both value and impact?

4. Do you understand the culture, history, and traditions behind those for whom you are designing?

5. Are you a disruptor/rule breaker?

6. Is there time, money, and opportunity to explore options and incorporate hands-on processes to stimulate creativity and innovation?

7. Have you immersed yourself in the sensory details of the project?

8. Why should anyone care about your content, design, or the experience you create?

9. Why will clients find your art/product/brand meaningful?

10. Can you take the time to examine every single layer or interaction, and carefully craft the touch points and make them memorable? The "deliciousness" is in the details!

Summary: Fast or Fastidious

When it comes to the products and services that we typically signify as having value, prestige, and even longevity, one single element factors into their creation: time. So why is it that design and the design processes, from ideation to development to implementation, are all happening on the fast track? And what are the implications of this? Our need for speed and our "I want it and I want it now" mindset have permeated our design processes. We must slow things down, simmer our thoughts, steep our strategies, and craft our ideas into existence. It takes time to do something exceptional. We do not want to be known as masters of mediocrity.

Time is the new currency. We must redefine it for ourselves and bring a holistic balance back into our existence. Busy cannot be our definition of success. We are enriched personally and professionally by the balance we bring to our efforts every day. It is important each day to take a few moments upfront and set intentions for the day, which helps prioritize activities, direct focus, and manage (and even gain) time.

Design discovery does not necessarily happen within a tight time framework. Lack of understanding of the design process has created unrealistic expectations. The trend toward "rapid prototyping" in order to generate, develop and produce products quickly eliminates opportunities for the creative play that goes arm-in-arm with exploration, discovery, and innovation.

Creativity takes time. Good ideas cannot be rushed. Sudden insights are not the norm. Creativity involves discovering, exploring, and organizing ideas. The key is to have the time to innovate and then work hard. Do not be tempted to rush the process and settle for mediocrity.

Rapid prototyping is a tool, not a process. The best place for it is in the ideation stage of the creative process. That is the stage where competing ideas or concepts are tested in order to select the one that best meets a critical criterion of requirements.

We must reclaim our power and redefine our relationship to process. People long for hands-on artisanship. With technology, everything we do today is done on screens. Where are the hands-on processes that give us a tangible knowledge of our craft? What does it benefit us or our clients if we have gained the whole world and lost touch with everything. There is value in doing things by hand, reaching beyond our known limits, and evolving to that next level of accomplishment and excellence. It is time to reintroduce craft and to stop sacrificing quality for competitiveness. It is time to rediscover listening, waiting, observing, experimenting, and reviewing for relevancy. And everything that we expect technology to do for us expeditiously, we must be able to replicate manually.

We are people designing for people.
Our art takes time.
Our senses and our handcraft are an inseparable part of the process.
We must embrace and embody our "turtle nature."

3 _Culture du Jour_

Distilling toward Discovery

Living in the NOW is a much different concept than wanting what we want right NOW. As I have already noted, today we live in a world of immediacy. Technology has transformed our interest and wonder in the new and the marvelous into an addiction for constant change. Our global metabolism has escalated to the velocity of "instantaneous."

Immediate gratification is our expectation. We have evolved into the Veruca Salt mindset of high expectation, which was fine for the spoiled and bratty Willy Wonka and the Chocolate Factory character, but is not so flattering for society as a whole.[9] Have we neglected the warning of Charlie Bucket's Grandpa Joe who said, "No good can ever come from spoiling a child like that...you mark my words."?

As a designer, artist, and a mother, I am committed to introducing my children to the discovery process that is the foundation of all creativity and originality. Building blocks, LEGOs, drawing, painting (even on walls), playing in the sandbox, building with sticks, sculpting with Play-Doh, hiking, interacting with nature and animals, and a myriad of other three-dimensional experiences all help shape the way my children perceive, learn, and create in their world. I loved it when my eldest son used toilet paper to represent car tracks, although initially I thought he was just making a mess in the house. I was excited when I realized the creativity behind his application. I knew he was living in the NOW, creating joyfully in the moment, as all children so instinctively do.

This same son mastered the iPad at six months of age. But I also want my child to have the "journey" of the discovery process. I want my child to know how to go to a library and look things up, follow threads of ideas, and make new connections. I don't want my children or anyone else to develop a tacit reliance on the computer, believing that everything it tells us is true.

Discovery is what gets left behind with all of our fingertip technology. We are detouring past important steps in the creative process: research, investigation, and exploration. Such instinct and initiative are being lost through disuse, even though it is during this course of the discovery process where valuable insights and connected ideas are waiting to be detected, unearthed, and identified. New York-based neurosurgeon Dr. Gopal Chopra emphasized the importance of the journey of discovery in an article written by John Brandon titled "Is Technology Making Us Less Human?"[10] According to Chopra, "Much of our character, creativity and moral fabric is built on the journey." Real-world activity is necessary for brain balance and wholeness, and our ability to respond appropriately to stimuli in our environment.

Are We Amputating Sensory Insights and Skills?

Consider Leonardo da Vinci's *Vitruvian Man*. This masterwork is a foray into the material and the metaphysical, a study in symmetry, proportion and beauty, an exploration of the relationship of parts that so perfectly create the whole being. In the "wholeness" there is the proportionality that informs the essence of art and architecture.

Are we so audacious as to seek to improve upon perfection? Why would we voluntarily limit and atrophy fundamental aspects of ourselves in favor of relying on technology, something so outside of ourselves, to manage our creative process? What if technology went dark one day? Would we still be able to function? The chaos that results from widespread power outages should be a wakeup call. We might be at a loss if forced to use our hands to create, draw, design, mend, repurpose, or craft. Are we losing our hands-on, tactile connection with the world, and our ability to think using our hands? Are we amputating our senses and all that makes us authentic artisanal beings?

In his work *Understanding Media,* author Marshall McLuhan (mid-twentieth-century pop culture guru who was the first to recognize the "global village") stated that adopting technology as an extension of ourselves does indeed amputate our natural gifts:

Every extension of mankind, especially technological extensions, has the effect of amputating or modifying some other extension... .With the arrival of electric technology, man extended, or set outside himself, a live model of the central nervous system itself. To the degree that this is so, it is a development that suggests a desperate and suicidal autoamputation, as if the central nervous system could no longer depend on the physical organs to be protective buffers against the slings and arrows of outrageous mechanism.[11]

Building on McLuhan's statement, Stacy Koosel of the Estonian Academy of Arts posits that we may be stressed beyond capacity and are unnaturally altered in mind, body, and action when we turn to other mediums to maintain balance and keep up the pace:

> *The extension of self in another medium can be the result of the stress of information overload and an increasingly demanding pace. Information overload and super stimulation of various kinds, will force the body to seek balance and maintain equilibrium—therefore other senses will be cut off or autoamputated by creating an extension. The extension of any sense will alter our thoughts and actions, as well as the way we perceive our environment and ourselves.*[12]

> **" "**
>
> Our over-reliance on technology can cloud our sensory judgment.
>
> —Dr. Neema Moraveji, Director of the Calming Technology Lab at Stanford University

We have evolved from a walking culture, to a car culture, to a culture that can go to the office without ever leaving home. And while we laud convenience and efficiency, we don't really study with any depth the impact of what technology costs us. As McLuhan says, "We have become people who regularly praise all extensions, and minimize all amputations." What of human interaction, exposure to the outdoors with all its sights, sounds, and colors, and our ability to navigate roads, directions, and changing circumstances?

Historically as a species, we collect information about our environment through our senses. Our very survival has been dependent on our acuity of sight, sound, touch, taste, and smell. The feedback transmitted through impulses to our brain helps regulate our balance and equilibrium, our ability to position and move our bodies in space. Like *Vitruvian Man,* our body is a perfect organism, with all senses working in concert to guide, inform, protect, and enrich us, and ensure our survival. Dr. Neema Moraveji, the director of the Calming Technology Lab at Stanford University, suggests that our over-reliance on technology can cloud our sensory judgment.[13] He says that the brain is an organ that learns through physiochemical and cognitive senses. "Without sufficient dynamism," says Moraveji, "the brain becomes focused on particular senses and inputs that are not representative of the natural world."

Our ability to perceive and translate human emotion becomes endangered as well. Although we are more "connected" than ever, our connection is to a screen and we are not engaged in interpersonal interactions which require us to perceive and translate visual and auditory cues. As Moraveji says, "We see only factual and textual information instead of an array of human emotions." Somehow, within our global village, technology is isolating us more and more and causing us to be less than the full complement of ourselves.

From Adept to Inept: Disconnected, Disposable, Disgruntled, and Disagreeable

The average American spends 11 hours daily with electronic media. Technology keeps us endlessly glued to screens, and, if we let it, it also relegates us to a cyber-reality social life. Social media is supplanting the coffee klatch and the happy hour. Without our awareness, our reliance on technology also chips away at our resourcefulness and good stewardship of natural resources. UK Science Editor Sarah Knapton, who writes for *The Telegraph,* says that we have become a lost generation who can no longer repair gadgets or appliances because we live in a disposable world.[14]

Knapton cites Danielle George, Professor of Radio Frequency Engineering at the University of Manchester, who observes that we are at a complete loss when something goes haywire in our perfectly ordered worlds. People, mostly those under 40 years of age, have an expectation that things will simply work, and when they stop working, no one knows what to do or how to fix the problem. We buy new and replace the old every time there is a hiccup in the electronics and technology we depend upon.

But if we decline to be absorbed by technology, and cultivate within us curiosity and initiative towards hands-on investigation, innovation, and creative engineering, we might realize ingenious opportunities to repurpose our technology and have the ability to do it ourselves. Prof. George suggests that there is now a large "maker" community thinking hard about new life for old gadgets and that the generation of young people has an expanding landscape of technology with which to be creative.

We all have the creative potential to be inventors, but do we have the initiative, the motivation, and above all, the patience? The downside of our culture of instant gratification is that we have forgotten how to wait, how to use time to percolate ideas. We no longer sit back and ponder possibilities, or give insights time to mature, manifest, and bear fruit. We are not born with patience. That is why it is referenced as a "virtue." It is practiced and cultivated. It is a process of mindfully taking the time to sit back, just be, and await an opportunity or a result. It is a conscious investment of time in hopes of producing a desired or more favorable outcome.

Goldfish, it turns out, have longer attention spans than people today, according to a recent study by Microsoft Corp.[15] Lest we be inclined to celebrate that observation, I consider it an indicator of distraction rather than a testimony to discernment. Another study illuminated the growing brevity of our patience.[16] More than three billion Google searches were conducted daily in 2012. When search results were slowed by 4/10 of a second, the number of searches executed were reduced by eight million. If pages didn't load in ten seconds, 50% of mobile users abandoned their searches. Nearly 25% of mobile users browsed the web only on their phone. If e-commerce sites did not load in three seconds, 40% of mobile shoppers abandoned their searches. For Amazon in 2012, which made about $67 million in sales daily, a one-second web page delay could cost the company more than $1.6 billion annually. Half of all consumers will not return to an establishment that keeps them waiting. And one out of five people admit to

The attention span of a goldfish is 9 seconds.

The attention span of a human is 8 seconds.

being rude to someone who provides slow service. In our impatience, we have sacrificed civility itself, an indicator of "civilized society."

The faster that technology forces us to live, the more we seek to control circumstances, and the more chaotic our lives seem to become when even one single element does not move at the speed of our expectation. I grow anxious just writing this. We have become a global society of multitaskers. Multitasking erodes our ability to pay focused, close attention, and this eventually eats away at traits such as patience, tenacity, judgment, and problem solving.[17]

> Multitasking actually reduces mental acuity and lowers IQ temporarily by 15%.

Impatience can have harmful and even serious consequences. It can affect our social, financial, emotional, and physical health and leave us feeling as if we are spinning out of control. It elevates stress, which leads to hypertension, obesity, heart disease, bad decisions, alcoholism, failed friendships, marriages, and business relationships. That's not to mention the fact that it is just a lousy way to feel. Who wants to be angry and on edge all the time? Yet, we have made multitasking a cultural imperative, a symbol of hard work and success. We base our reward systems on institutionalized distraction, which is harmful to beings at every level of their existence: physically, emotionally, mentally and spiritually. Multitasking actually reduces mental acuity and lowers IQ temporarily by 15%, reduces productivity ($650 billion annually in the United States) by interrupting flow and momentum, contributes to premature aging, impairs judgment, heightens anxiety, and increases the number of mistakes made. The brain just isn't designed for this activity. Judge for yourself the next time you are overloaded with "to-dos" and discover you have become forgetful due to the impact of stress on your short-term memory.

One Small Wafer-Thin Mint;
Say No before You Blow

Remember Mr. Creosote from Monty Python's film *The Meaning of Life*? This fictional character stuffed himself to capacity with food, and at the urging of the waiter, also devoured a small, thin mint, thereby tipping the gastronomic scale and causing himself to explode.[18] The average adult today should be wearing a sign that says DANGER: CONTENTS UNDER PRESSURE.

We are a global society of multitaskers, stressed from trying to do too many things at once and relying on the lightning speed of technology to help us keep pace with our time clocks and calendars. Our plates are overfull. Each of us individually is trying to accomplish tasks numerous enough to be delegated to an entire village. So it should come as no surprise that small children are not the only ones having meltdowns these days. Our levels of anxiety over things past and future have ramped up beyond all that is healthy and wise. According to the Anxiety and Depression Association of America, anxiety disorders affect 40 million adults age 18 and older in the United States (2016).[19]

How can we be at peace in our minds, bodies, and spirits when we constantly feel that the devil is at the door and tasks are looming and left undone? How can we "be here now," when we are busy trying to be everywhere else at once. Multitasking negates Presence. It flies in the face of the creative's need to be present in the NOW. Contemporary philosopher/teacher Eckhart Tolle equates our "loss of the NOW" to a "loss of BEING."[20] If we are regularly not focusing our consciousness on the present moment, we gravitate toward a deep state of unconsciousness when challenges occur, and anxiety and unhappiness become our constant companions.

Perhaps we have forgotten that we are the ones in control. We have personal power, free will, and a voice. We can set our own pace, if we choose. And since we created technology, we can decide whether we will use it to unlock opportunities for us, or if we will let it push us into a state of being where we do not recognize ourselves and are out of touch with our own essence. We do not have to "eat the mint." Allan Lokos, founder of The Community Meditation Center in New York, reminds us that technology is external, while impatience is internal.[21] He says that because of all that we do with technology, there is more potential to be impatient, but we must realize that these miraculous devices are just tools. They are not our life. We must use them only to get the information we need, and then turn them off and live our lives with balance and purpose. Lokos advises, "Let technology work at its pace. We need to work at our pace, as human beings." [22]

There are benefits to learning patience and delaying gratification when what we really want to do is act on impulse and ingratiate ourselves with the next big thing. What price do we pay for our "infobesity lifestyle," for the sugared promise of absorbing yet another thin mint? It is so not worth the cost in this age where technology is at its zenith. In theory, technology is supposed to liberate us and give us more free time, and yet we have a poverty of time. During a session at the Annual Women's Forum in France in 2013, speakers Delphine Remy-Boutang, the founder and CEO of The Social Bureau, and Christophe Aguiton, researcher at the Orange Labs claimed that due to the acceleration of our lives led by the acceleration of technology, people are trying to live 10 lives at once, with all of the cumulative stress and anxiety inherent in that condensed lifestyle.[23] Yes, we are under relentless pressure to sample all of the good things in life. But perhaps less really is more. It is time to focus again on the quality of our existence and all that we do, and not the quantity of stuff that implodes our lives. The outcome of 40 years of Stanford research on choosing discipline over satisfying impulse revealed that the ability to delay gratification is critical for success.[24] People who master this self-control typically have better social skills, better responses to stress, lower levels of substance abuse and less tendency toward obesity.

As we grapple with the challenge of how best to manage technology's onslaught, we cannot deny its effect on our global lifestyle. We live in a culture of NOW, a culture of mass production and mass consumption where we are constantly upgrading and demanding more and more in less and less time. And to keep in step with our expanding appetite, the value of all that we covet diminishes. Time is our taskmaster, and at the pace of chaotic, we adopt an attention deficit dynamic and choose fast food over home-cooked meals, instant ramen over späetzle, cheese food over aged cheddar, Mp3 over symphony, and television over theatre. I too am guilty. I found my time and budget savior in the "fast, cheap and easy" instant ramen noodles that sustained me as I put myself through design school. Expediency and affordability can make products, services, and experiences attractive. We forget the process of time and craft and all that they contribute to a complete experience. Not only have we amputated our senses, we have amputated our ability to appreciate and enjoy the fullness and depth of special events and milestone moments. We compromise, we settle, and we accept the mass-produced and the superficial over the original, the crafted, and the authentic.

Do you recall Aesop's fable about the lioness, who during a debate

> The outcome of 40 years of Stanford research on choosing discipline over satisfying impulse revealed that the ability to delay gratification is critical for success.

between animals over who deserved the most credit for having the greatest number of offspring, declared that while she only gave birth to one, it was the king of beasts. Value and quality are in the worth, not the quantity. And the worth of anything is contingent on the time and thoughtful creation invested that impart uniqueness. While we are the creators of the technology and time scarcity conundrum, we are also the only ones who can and must manage our participation in the chaos in order to retain, rekindle and embody a passionate commitment to craftsmanship.

And so the race begins. The tension between quality and quantity, between legendary and mediocre, between discovering, thinking, and creating versus simply doing is being tested and challenged. As artisans and designers of products and experiences, we must set the focus and the foundation, do the right thing, and hearken back to our Artisan's Oath (see Chapter 1) where we commit to mindfully create premiere products and experiences for people and our clients. As we rekindle our passion for artisanship and craft, we must be ready for the byproducts that such a revolution of high standards, attention to detail, and precise execution will bring: gratitude, appreciation, patience, peacefulness, civility, and wellness. Are we ready?

Case Study: Craig Sewing,
TV Host of *The American Dream Show*

Product, purpose and persona are all essential elements in crafting a visible and values-driven brand. Craig Sewing, CEO and Executive Producer of *The American Dream Show* has mindfully created a distinctively positive television show that engages, educates and empowers his audience. While feeding the public appetite for "culture du jour" might temporarily drive a show's popularity, ratings, and media frenzy, Craig is not another shouting voice in the ratcheting volume of opinion news shows and media personalities. He has not entered the fray of negative news, divisive attitudes, or narcissistic popular culture, nor does he contribute to the roar of what's wrong in America. Instead, he chooses to focus on messages of hope, support, authenticity, positive action, and real and balanced human connection.

This San Diego-based television and radio personality grew up in the Midwest, has a background in finance and real estate, and is a successful entrepreneur. As someone who likes to build and create, Craig has amassed an impressive network of professionals across markets and industries, whose expertise he solicits on behalf of his listeners. A tireless consumer advocate, Craig invites his audience to seek advice and input from his team of financial and real estate experts and others. This no-strings consulting empowers his listeners to obtain the direction and insights necessary to move them toward their own American dream.

Craig views the negative media and reality television, with their cutthroat competitiveness and whining entitlement, as a deteriorating factor in our thinning cultural fabric. He champions new ways of seeing, encourages new ways to compete, and advocates for meaningful endeavor out of which evolves happiness and success. Success, according to Craig, is not defined by money. Rather, it is defined by your state of happiness, excitement, contentment and fulfillment in the moment. He lives the ideals he promotes.

Conscious of a world of distraction and wanting to train his mind to focus productively, Craig took his appreciation for Eastern philosophy to a personal level. This activist for positive messaging developed his own self-improvement program for harnessing his abundant energies and calming his subconscious mind. He employed meditation and working out to help him think clearly and decisively and use his mind effectively. He learned to balance his persona as a public figure with his need for a private personal life, managing expectations, drawing boundaries, and employing certain rules of engagement. Inspired by his own evolution and growth, he became an advocate for personal development practices. Rather than preach, he led his team by example, encouraging them to explore their own tools for self-empowerment and personal growth.

Craig feels that crafting his own development helps him to develop his craft. His daily meditation practice gives him clarity of vision and purpose as he approaches each day. In this modern world of "bigger and faster" where velocity is multiplied exponentially by technology, Craig depends on meditation and reflection to keep him centered. While technology has its benefits as a tool for connection and information access, Craig fears that constant immersion in virtual worlds is causing people to lose all sense of what is real and reduces human connectivity and productivity.

Large segments of society have unwittingly become trapped on their phones and computer screens, unable and unwilling to look away, needing the instant gratification of the next Tweet, Facebook post, email update or text message. The resultant anxiety, depression and isolation caused by lack of authentic human contact or real relationship building poses threats to mental health. Craig would rather see kids outside playing sports rather than hiding in basements playing virtual shooting and carjacking games. And he would rather see people communicating face to face, phone-free, rather than conducting their personal and business lives via little screens. He believes that a meditation practice can help people distinguish noise versus signal and counter the anxiety and disorienting disconnection that technology produces in our increasingly faster-paced world.

Passion and enthusiasm radiate from this intense and authentic personality who faces issues head on, speaks bluntly and unapologetically, stays true to his core values, and is ever ready to lend a hand to lift others up. Again, he leads by example, demonstrating how a significant life is one crafted with balance, values, purpose and conviction, and lived out loud in the real-world with an attitude of grace and helpfulness, and with the meaning that comes from real connection and honest productivity. This just might be the recipe for realizing the perfect American dream.

Summary: Culture du Jour

Technology has nurtured our addiction to constant change. It has taken us from living in the "now" and engaging three-dimensional, real-world experiences to expecting immediate gratification. With fingertip technology, the journey of "discovery" recedes. We detour past important steps in the creative process: research, investigation and exploration. It is this journey that makes us whole and wholly human. It develops our senses, builds our character, and stimulates creativity.

The human body is a perfect organism whose senses serve to guide, inform, protect, and enrich our lives while ensuring our survival. It is important to question if we are amputating our senses through our dependence on technology. Our brain learns through physiochemical and cognitive sensing, and now we are asking it to rely on input that is not from the natural world. Face-to-face human interaction also suffers. With an average of 11 hours of electronic media daily, we have become isolated, and our ability to perceive and translate human emotion is endangered.

Should technology go dark someday, would we know how to function?

Would we have the attention span and patience to observe and create? We live at technology's rapid pace and try to control circumstances. But when even one element does not move at the pace of expectation, we experience chaos and anxiety. We multitask, and do not focus on what is happening in the present moment, which reduces our mental acuity and productivity, erodes patience, tenacity, judgment and problem solving. We become stressed, angry, unhealthy, and unable to maintain successful relationships.

We must remember that we are in control, not technology. We have personal power and can decide to set our own pace. Technology is a tool we can shut on and off so that we can live more balanced lives. Delaying gratification helps us develop better social skills and healthier lifestyles and responses to stress. When we slow down our pace, we can more fully appreciate the fullness and depth of every moment. Our instant gratification culture, with its mass production and consumption, has diminished our concept of value. We accept "fast, cheap and easy," over "crafted and authentic" because we have forgotten how the process of time and craft contribute to experience. By better managing our participation in technology's "time scarcity" chaos, we can live more authentic lives. By leaving the race for a more mindful pace, we can fully embrace and embody craftsmanship and quality, and the accompanying appreciation and joy.

4 *Craftsmanship*

A Tradition of Focused Expertise:
Then and Now

Craftsmanship is the creation of something through the mindful application of care, skills, technique, style, ingenuity, and quality of work. The term *craftsmanship* denotes the perfection of a discipline that employs hands-on processes in the creation of art; writing; stone, wood, metal, textile, glass, and other handcrafts; and other labors of passion.

As consumers, we still covet goods identified as being Made in Italy or Made in Germany over those Made in USA or Made in China. Some key aesthetic sets those goods apart, and distinguishes them from a domestic product or something that may be a mass-produced knockoff. I believe the "draw" is the belief that someone skilled in a craft "tradition" took the time and applied carefully focused attention and hands-on expertise to create a beautiful finished product. But time is money, and in order to be a consumer/collector of crafted goods, you must be willing to pay the artisan price tag.

In his book *Shop Class as Soul Craft,* Matthew Crawford states that Craftsmanship requires focusing on something for a long period of time and delving into the nature of it for the purpose of understanding it fully and "getting it right." [25] There is no instantaneous execution of effort resulting in the magical appearance of a well-crafted item. Deliberation delivers, eventually. But, while Craftsmanship entails "learning to do one thing really well," this is at odds with the "cutting-edge institutions" of the new capitalism. In the new economy, the focus is on potential and not achievement. Rather than refining a set of skills, people are urged to constantly learn new things. We've become a society that "knows about" but does not necessarily "know how." And the consumer mindset in this disposable economy runs parallel, where people hunger for the next new thing to replace what is still functioning and viable.

Our manual and technical skills required ongoing encounters with the material world and a developing knowledge of patterns, causes and behaviors. This heightened our cognitive skills, our ability to problem solve and innovate, and deepened our understanding of the "nature of things." We were self-sufficient, which came in handy as the pioneering population moved into the far reaches of our vast nation and settled into building communities, raising families and shaping livelihoods. The advent of assembly line manufacturing turned artisanship and aptitude upside down by making technology and machines the doers, and people merely the conveyor belt monitors and product disseminators.

Computers supplanted creative cognition, and with our hands severed from their source of dimensional thought and inspiration in doing, we became a nation of robots and automatons sporting repetitive stress injuries. We have pace without presence, and all product is imitation, with origination that is mold and template, and not original. It is good for us to remember that hands that work are attached to and help develop brains that think, coordinate, and create. As Greek philosopher Anaxagoras said, "It is by having hands that man is the most intelligent of animals."

A Cultural Perspective

I grew up in Malaysia, which, although it is considered a third-world country, has a rich culture of artisanship and hands-on processes. In fact, the hands that touch and provide consumer goods are largely "known" to the average person. For example, I grew up with farm-to-table dining. We would go to the market and select a live chicken. The farmer would dispatch and de-feather the chicken, and prep the meat. My mom would then take the chicken home to cook us curry, with paste made from the mortar and pestle, and coconut milk freshly squeezed from the husk.

During my childhood, there was only one grocery store in Penang, where one could enjoy air conditioning, and find packaged hot dogs. But the majority of daily goods were purchased at local sundry shops, owned by families for generations, which sold anything from feather dusters to tiger balms. Here one could find the exquisite Malaysian Kebaya dress crafted with handmade lace, hand-painted silk, and adorned with brocade or floral pattern embroidery. There were artisans selling handmade swords (keris), rattan baskets, handmade foods wrapped in banana leaf, and spice merchants pounding their aromatic wares on mortar and pestle. Soy milks were freshly made, and unpasteurized cow's milk was sold from the back of motorbikes, with the milk man screaming out "susu" to announce his goods.

A craftsperson is anyone who has spent much of their life passionately perfecting, pushing, experimenting, and connecting with their craft in pursuit of either finding new ways to make their work better, or helping to enhance the lives of others.

This heady, unfiltered process of merchants and customers was so direct and honest. We all knew the fish monger, the vegetable guy, the butcher, and the vendor with the best cili padi (a type of spicy chili pepper that is an essential ingredient in Malaysian cooking). Such a "system," such a market "scene" feels chaotic to most Westerners. But for me it was rich with lessons, longstanding traditions, and culture. My first sales lessons came in the form of old ladies and women with their children tagging along, screaming at each other, haggling over pennies as they vied for the best fish. This rudimentary process helped form my deep appreciation for small business owners, workers, anyone who builds with their hands, and anyone who wakes up at 4:00 in the morning to work an 18-hour day supporting their families, and doing it all with such pride. My love for craft blossomed here in this hub of activity, culture, connection, and family cottage traditions.

A Love Affair

The word *craft* can be quite misleading. It might conjure thoughts of gluing stars and affixing photographs in scrapbooks. When I think of craft, I think of stonemasons who chisel marble or granite, master sushi chefs, the premières, "les petites mains," glassblowers, watchmakers, carpenters, cabinet makers, and on and on.

A craftsperson is anyone who has spent much of their life passionately perfecting, pushing, experimenting, and connecting with their craft in pursuit of either finding new ways to make their work better, or helping to enhance the lives of others. This relentless pursuit can be skewed and misconstrued. In writing about the documentary *Jiro Dreams of Sushi*, a film about a renowned sushi chef, film critic Roger Ebert called it a "portrait of tunnel vision."[26] He offered the following observation:

> While watching it, I found myself drawn into the mystery of this man. Are there any unrealized wishes in his life? Secret diversions? Regrets? If you find an occupation you love and spend your entire life working at it, is that enough? Standing behind his counter, Jiro notices things. Some customers are left-handed, some right-handed. That helps determine where they are seated at his counter. As he serves a perfect piece of sushi, he observes it being eaten. He knows the history of that piece of seafood. He knows his staff has recently started massaging an octopus for 45 minutes and not half an hour, for example. Does he search a customer's eyes for a signal that this change has been an improvement? Half an hour of massage was good enough to win three Michelin stars.

You realize the tragedy of Jiro Ono's life is that there are not, and will never be, four stars.[27]

To me, not being awarded four stars is not a tragedy. To me that is art. Expectation of reward is not a motivation for craft. The reward is in the doing, learning, growing, and pushing boundaries. It is intrinsic to the pursuit of excellence, a journey that often only a fellow artisan can appreciate. Process, time, effort, love, sacrifice, passion, and a willingness to be vulnerable to criticism and even hostile feedback all go into creating something for someone else to enjoy and appreciate. Sharing your soul with the world through the work that you create from nothing is craft. It is also design as well as any endeavor to which you give yourself fully.

Why Do We Craft?

We Love What We Do

As a designer, my work is also my passion, need, and drive to create order, form, functional excellence, beauty, and enhanced well-being. For me, design is a serotonin-stimulating invitation to problem solving. The more I do, the more I discover that there is so much more to know and understand. Design lets me exercise my creative muscles and refine my discerning eyes, strategic approaches, and technical discipline. I get to play in the world of "what might be" if I make certain choices, and I get to balance scenarios and solutions and forecast outcomes and benefits. Craft and the art and science of creating lets us be explorers, lets us be the archaeologists and excavators of our own interiors, intuitions, skills and ingenuity, and makes us mindful of our awesome responsibility for what we create in the world. As a craftsperson with design as my medium, I find that my work is like breathing. I cannot NOT do it. I ply my craft in all aspects of my life and living, whether I am working with clients, raising my family, cultivating friendships, taking vacations, or exploring new interests. My craft represents connection, life, and the mystical matrix of all that is, in all its dimensionality. I cannot help but be mesmerized by it.

We Care to Contribute

My craft is both a head trip and an ego boost because as a designer, I know that people in my field are key players in creating what others experience in the world. My craft is also a call to action for accountability. Like most designers, I care to create a better world. Can any of us ever really tire from sincerity and purity of purpose? I realize the dimensional impact of my work, from the surface and tangible materialism, to the emotional, economic, environmental, political and sociocultural effects. Everything designers put into the world carries a message and a signature. Message, signature, and impact all begin from the moment we have the inspiration to create. This is true no matter what or how you craft. The very act, the very process of executing your craft is a contribution in and of itself. It builds on and adds as much to the tradition and legacy of your discipline (for better or worse) as it does to the individuals and industries it influences and serves.

We Seek to Create Value through Experience and Work

Value is as much a verb as it is a noun. Every time someone creates something, part of their hope is that whatever is created will not only have purpose, it will have meaning. The time, energy, skill, and materials that go into crafting something all contribute to the economic value (and/or cost) of the product, and in a more aesthetic sense, to the way in which the product is esteemed. Craftspeople with true passion and integrity work tirelessly, constantly perfecting, refining, re-envisioning, and learning. Their dedication to their art translates directly into the work that they do, and often results in achievements in their field. Designers who set benchmarks and standards for excellence will tell you that even more satisfying than all the rewards and accolades they earn is the realization that their hard work is valued and appreciated. Beauty is only seen by those who can appreciate it. And that appreciation, that sense of valuing something from its surface to its soul requires acknowledgment and awareness of the process of creation. Neither Rome or Value were built in a day.

We Want Others to Appreciate Craft and Its Value

In my profession, we champion "doers." As a designer, I value originality born of creative thinking, innovation, expertise and skillful execution. I know what it takes to do something well and I want others to genuinely appreciate the backstory behind the deliverable. That all begins with each of us when we engage our craft, and it trickles down. We must examine our own motives and manifesto for creating in this world. Once we are on board with our own principles and agenda, it is beneficial to teach clients and customers to understand and value our process, knowing that the end result will be a product or experience with tenor, longevity, solid worth, pleasing aesthetics, and real purpose.

Our work is our legacy and our reason for doing. It reflects squarely on us just as it mirrors the world back to itself and strives to reflect a desirable, appealing, and saleable image. It is important for each of us to share what we know and to help educate others so that they can make informed choices. Elitism in a knowledge base, whether it's design, healthcare, engineering, etc., is a dangerous precedent and creates a culture of dependency where people will simply accept what is offered. How much better and more meaningful it is to teach people the "why and how" of what there is to value and have them stand behind and support the "doing." When we cultivate appreciation of craft, we avoid the pitfalls of ego and the alluring narcissism of "solo" accomplishment and can relish the satisfaction of a job well done.

We Care to Create Great Products, Services, Businesses, Experiences, Brands, and Relationships

With the rise of mass production in our societies, the need for dedicated mastery in our professions is greater now than ever before. The atrophy of craft traditions (and the technical skills and sense of individuation they provided) has left people more reactive than discerning when presented with new ideas, products, and services. The design environment is deluged with images and offerings, where everyone claims to be an authority knowing that most people are not equipped with the tools for validation that enable seeing past glitter and charisma to test foundation and solid integrity. The true creative wants to do more than innovate a great original work, execute a great sales job, or be recognized as a solutions avatar. Yes, as craftspeople, we want to create amazing products, brands, and services that have integrity, longevity, reliability, accountability, life-enhancing benefits, economic and environmental resourcefulness, and that are innovative and timely. But the crux of craftsmanship is about so much more than building tangibles or intangibles, or interpreting design environments. It's about more than leading people to "utopian" possibilities. It's about building relationships and defining together how best to live. This fascinating and fluid connection with one another is at the core of anything worth doing.

A craftsperson can be an artisan, a musician, a poet, an architect, a doctor, an electrician, a carpenter, a maker, or even the guy who has fried noodles for the last 20 years on the streets of Hanoi.

Revive Your Inner Craftsperson

Do you feel you are called to be a craftsperson? Before you say no, either out of humility or an unwillingness to be a pit bull-creative worrying a project bone, let's first examine and understand the attributes of a craftsman. These aspirational attributes cut across all of the arts and disciplines:

- A passion for excellence and a drive toward mastery

- Immersion in practice with an astute focus on craft

- A willingness to sacrifice time, money, and personal pleasure for the work

- The ability to view failure as a step in the process of "becoming"

- A drive toward constant learning

- A confident integrity tempered by humility

- Accountability for and ownership of one's work

- An unshakeable belief in product and purpose

- Respect for tradition and the value of process

- The doing is the reward

A craftsperson can be an artisan, a musician, a poet, an architect, a doctor, an electrician, a carpenter, a maker, or even the guy who has fried noodles for the last 20 years on the streets of Hanoi. Craftsmanship is a pledge—to dedicate oneself to mastering a profession, to be the master of something one is passionate about instead of being the master of none. It constitutes a call to ownership and accountability, a call to learn and renew in order to offer clients and customers the very best.

Craftspeople are builders and makers. They build businesses, buildings, technology, and services, and they enable others to build dreams and make them a reality. They are inspiring beacons and master motivators. And they do it with ease, because their passion and their years of dedication, their 10,000 hours of practice (thank you Malcolm Gladwell) enabled them to know what rules to break, what new rules to create, and guided them to ultimately create new experiences, new products, and new services, better, quicker, faster, and more effectively, cost-efficiently, and sustainably.[28]

The life experiences of craftspeople help cultivate their discerning tastes and hone their instincts and acumen. They know the difference between good versus great, silver versus gold, winning the right races, and letting go when it's time. When crisis hits, they know how to navigate with ease, because they've seen it a thousand times. They are able to manage priorities and negotiate sticky situations with integrity and conviction. They know what truly matters and that although doing the right thing may be the hardest course, it is the only way. They know that life is beyond dollars and cents, and that business is in fact personal. After all, they have done it 10,000 times. They have cultivated that intimacy with their practice, and they know what it takes to build a world-class team, brand, and business. They are aware that time is of the essence and yet craft cannot be forced, manipulated, or rushed. They know that not all things are black and white. There are grey areas to investigate—to find the next big aha moment, and to nurture an idea into something great. They also know that there is no single way of making things. There can be a hundred other ways to deliver you a piece of art. They have this awareness because they have experienced, through trial and error and practice, what to do and not to do in order to save time without sacrificing quality.

These abilities reflect dedication and the persistent application of ritual conventions, practices and processes that peel away the layers of all that would cloud clarity, understanding, and pure achievement. These skills can only be cultivated through mastering craft. These qualities may be found or developed in you.

Case Study: Baume & Mercier

Baume & Mercier is internationally recognized as the seventh oldest Swiss watchmaking brand. For almost two centuries, the craftsmen at Baume & Mercier have maintained a heritage of design perfection as they manufacture only watches of the highest quality and reliability. Each piece possesses a timeless elegance, which means it can be worn and enjoyed for years to come no matter the purchase date. Baume & Mercier is proud that so many of its watches are purchased as gifts to celebrate special moments or occasions. The brand's relevancy rests in its being closely associated with that special moment, whether it happened last week or 15 years ago.

The average age of this classic watchmaker's craftsmen is 40 years. Within the team, there are older more experienced watchmakers whose role is to transmit their knowledge and savoir-faire to young watchmakers who have completed training in the region's watchmaking classes. A true master craftsman isn't just the individual who works on the watches, but also the techniques, skills, and approach to producing a watch that possesses both heritage and legacy. In other words, craftsmanship can be part of the brand's very fabric.

The Maison Baume & Mercier has always preferred to manage all the stages of development internally in order to preserve the brand's DNA and the design aesthetic codes, and also the perfect quality, reliability and durability of its creations. The organizational model is structured to include all the necessary skills: marketing teams, in-house studio design, and the Maîtrise d'œuvre, in Les Brenets, where the watchmaking workshops are located.

Historically, watchmaking was developed in the calm countryside and mountainous regions, especially in the Swiss Jura. The long winters, when the activity in the fields was less active, provided a suitable environment of calm and concentration for the development of watchmaking activity. Today, the company is dedicated year-round to the production and maintenance of its timepieces and continues to benefit from a source of talented watchmakers available in the region.

Technology has helped the design team further the design process with the introduction of tools like 3D printers. Rather than sending a drawing out for a model to be created, which can take months, designers input their paper designs to create a CAD design. Then a 3D printer produces a watch model overnight that undergoes intense review by seeing, wearing and touching it. This wonderful addition to the process enables Baume & Mercier to speed up the production timetable.

Balancing creativity and artisanship with the technical precision that fine watchmaking demands is indeed a delicate balance. Ultimately, each watch must tell precise time, and if there are small complications, they must work as designed and created. The design team works closely with the design marketing team to ensure this essential balance is struck and that each watch is both technically precise and pleasing to the eyes and wrists.

Cultivating inspiration, creativity, and the desire for constant improvement and perfection is inherent within each of Baume & Mercier's designers and craftsmen. The talented team members are students of the world. They travel, attend art shows, see live theatre, read books, enjoy magazines, and visit a variety of cultural institutions in order to foster inspiration and keep their creative juices flowing. When they begin a new design project, they often create mood boards to capture color, texture, photos, materials and anything that will inspire the spirit and design of the watch.

The design team starts with hand-drawn pencil sketches that often take their inspiration from watches in the company archives. Designers use the past to influence and inspire the future. Each watch is born from the watchmakers' passion and from their tireless quest for perfection. Above and beyond conceptualizing a unique shape, the process may involve inventing a case, a dial, a mechanism, a strap, or a bracelet.

For students aspiring to be fine watchmakers, Baume & Mercier recommends they contact the FHH (Foundation of Fine Watchmaking or Fondation de la Haute Horlogerie), which offers many fine watchmaking classes. It is a beautiful way to get started and interact with some of the finest training programs offered by the world of watches.

Balancing social media and new technologies with fine craftsmanship requires thought and care. Properly presenting a quality craft to a receptive market requires insight, strategy and terrific storytelling. Baume &

Mercier watches are not just utilitarian devices for telling time. Rather, they are markers of history, memories, and all that is important to the wearers. Social media is the ideal platform for sharing such stories. So often customers proactively post pictures of themselves giving or receiving a Baume & Mercier, and it is easy to see the moments that are being celebrated by the atmosphere and expressions. While the stories have been shared for more than 187 years, they now can be streamed to people instantly and garner immediate inspiration.

As a global brand that cares to remain relevant and recognizable to consumers, Baume & Mercier understands the necessity of being cognizant of the cultural nuances and practices of the markets that carry its products. The launch of Promesse is a good example. In China, Baume & Mercier made sure to offer a reference with a red strap that was introduced around Chinese New Year.

In the world of watches, being old is actually quite prestigious and honorable. Baume & Mercier is committed to respecting the fine work of its founders, their motto, and all that has contributed to the brand's success. The company keeps one eye focused on the future in order to remain relevant to the current and future customers of the brand. It is a true balance of the brand's rich history, along with the creativity and innovation of today's collections that makes Baume & Mercier a leader in offering classic timepieces for men and women.

Summary: Craftsmanship

Craftsmanship is the high art of creative excellence involving the mindful application of care, skills, technique, style, ingenuity, and quality work. America was once a nation of craftspeople and "doers" who had the cognitive skills to problem solve and innovate, and who understood the "nature of things." But assembly line manufacturing and technology buried our fluency in craftsmanship and relegated it to novelty. In our disposable economy, consumers hunger for the next new thing and readily discard what is still functioning and viable.

When I was growing up in Malaysia, the majority of daily goods were purchased at local sundry shops owned by families for generations. The relationship between merchants and customers was direct and honest. In this milieu of longstanding traditions, activity and connection, my love for craftsmanship blossomed. A craftsperson is anyone who has committed their life to perfecting, experimenting with and plying their craft in order to deliver a great experience and make the world a better place. Expectation of reward is not a motivation for craft. The reward is in the doing, learning, growing and pushing of boundaries.

Craftspeople love what they do. The art and science of creating lets craftspeople exercise creativity and discernment and develop strategies and technical disciplines. We excavate our own interiors, intuitions, skills and ingenuity, and understand our responsibility for what we create in the world. Craft is contribution, and everything we create carries both a message and a signature. We work tirelessly perfecting, refining, re-envisioning and learning, and find our biggest reward in knowing that our work and its backstory are valued and appreciated. It benefits everyone when clients and customers understand and value our process and know what it takes to create a product or experience with tenor, longevity, purpose and worth. The very crux of craftsmanship is not simply about creating something or leading people to utopian possibilities. It's about building relationships and defining how best to live.

True craftspeople possess the following inspirational attributes:

- A passion for excellence and a drive toward mastery

- Immersion in practice with an astute focus on craft

- A willingness to sacrifice time, money, and personal pleasure for the work

- The ability to view failure as a step in the process of "becoming"

- A drive toward constant learning

- A confident integrity tempered by humility

- Accountability and ownership for one's work

- An unshakeable belief in product and purpose

- Respect for tradition and the value of process

- The doing is the reward

We are builders and makers who inspire and motivate. Our life experiences contribute to our artistic development and our realization that life is more than dollars and cents; there are 10,000 ways of doing things, and business is personal. We manage priorities, embody integrity, decline to rush process, and nurture ideas into greatness. These qualities can be found and developed in you.

5   *Wisdom + Passion = Purpose*

Balance Passion with Planning

New experiences and activities inform and enlighten me, and breathe fresh inspiration into my creative spirit. No long ago, I watched the movie *"Dior and I."* [29] What a beautiful film—not only because of its exploration into the almost lost art of couture, craft, beauty, and design, but also because it focused on the people behind great brands, and the interplay of teamwork between masters and apprentices.

With the changing business landscape, there are only a few great couture houses left—Chanel and Dior—where every bead, every stitch is made by hand. No machine production takes place. As I sat there watching the documentary that featured five people gathered around a table, undoing beads and stitching by hand, and rushing for the next deadline without sacrificing quality, I was almost in tears.

I do not know how to explain this feeling, but it reminded me of when I had just given birth to my second child, who arrived seven weeks early. The day after I left the hospital, a CEO called me and asked me when I would complete the 20 sets of hand-painted illustrations he had contracted me to create for him. Without even thinking twice, I sat down for an entire week, eight hours a day, in between trying to regain my strength and attempting to breast-feed, I hand water-colored 20 paintings for him. So when I viewed *"Dior and I,"* I connected with those premieres and les petite mains on that film, and their unquestioning dedication to their craft.

As I reflect on that one lost week with my newborn, and the amount of love I poured into the work I produced, I have to wonder: what did I gain, and what did I give up? What did it cost me? I knew I had gone too far. Much to my disappointment, two weeks after I submitted the project, those hand-painted illustrations didn't survive long on the home page of the new website. Half of the hand-painted watercolor drawings, which amounted to the time I took away from my newborn in order to produce work that I felt was truly important and would significantly and positively impact my client's business, didn't really make a dent at all. The drawings were taken down after a couple of weeks of A/B testing, with data showing a faster conversion rate for a home page. That was the moment I realized that I had been blinded by this love affair I have with craft. That was when I understood that while every client with whom I work receives the same dedication and relentless pursuit of craft, quality, and excellence, and while no one should ever doubt my company's ability to produce amazing work, that is not the point of craft.

Craftsmanship speaks of artistry, dedication, commitment, laser attention to detail, and a generous allocation of time spent creating. Many of us are like Da Vinci in our own way, yet we are trying to find our optimal path in this modern, technology-driven world. We must navigate between staying relevant and staying inspired. We must meet the demands of modern "cheaper, faster, easier" processes while retaining our love for our craft, and dedicating the time needed to master it. We are trying not to compromise quality over quantity, our own value and ethics over "business is not personal." We strive to do what is right for our family, and still balance the demands of a competitive workforce. Our passion for our craft, our desire to create, is so deep inside us. Still we recognize that we must mindfully balance our heady love of creating with wisdom and purpose so that we do not lose sight of our goal and priorities. We must have a plan that brings the head and the heart together. We must have a deep understanding of who we are as craftspeople, and why we do what we do.

Know Yourself, Inside and Out

Get ready to take good notes. You are about to embark on a journey into your own motivations and deepest needs. You will be mindfully mapping answers to penetrating questions and looking for patterns and purpose. This is a journey of discovering, unleashing, and rediscovering yourself. It is all part of the artisanship journey. It is how we keep grounded in our values, and how we manifest them into works that can benefit others at both a micro and macro scale.

When we gaze into our interiors, when we truly excavate our core, we find that as true artists, our love and passion for our craft resides there, in our hearts, in our very DNA. We create from the inside out. And all design and craft decisions we find ourselves presented with must be assessed and driven by the resonance of our hearts. They must align with what is true to us at the deepest levels of our being.

Author, ethnographer, and leadership expert Simon Sinek popularized a concept known as the Golden Circle which starts with the very basic question at the center of the circle: *Why*.[30] *Why* asks you to consider your purpose, your cause, or your belief. *Why* do you do what you do? *Why* do you get out of bed in the morning, and *why* should anyone care? It is the main motivator, the main driver of all action. Creatives must ask themselves *why* they create, *why* they ply their craft. According to the rule of the Golden Circle, once you identify the *why* at the core, your purpose then radiates out to the *How,* and then finally to the *What* of what you do. Expression, in all its forms, journeys from the inside out. It all comes from the heart.

Consider, as Sinek did, why someone would sacrifice their life for others. First responders—people in the military, police, and firefighting professions—are trained to follow commands. While they may be trained (a brain activity) to do their job and obey orders, it takes real heart to walk into a fire or the line of fire to save a buddy, a stranger, or maybe even someone you detest. I believe that years of training and conditioning enable these strong men and women to make split-second decisions in moments of extreme stress, facilitating their ability to think strategically and yet with their heart.

Sinek believes that communicating from the inside out drives behavior. People don't buy what you do. They buy *why* you do it. The goal then is to do business with people who believe what you believe. Here aspiration and inspiration come together. Creator and consumer come together through resonance, appreciation, the perception of a common wavelength. There is a gut recognition that something "feels right" about what you are doing, and this "sensing" informs and guides action.

Starting with why helps us frame the issue/problem and approach at a 50,000-foot level. It helps us set our intentions.

Asking the question *Why* helps you shift your observations and broaden perspectives to see the world outside of your bubble. It promotes discovery and leads you to follow golden threads to real issues and true meaning. It reveals the foundation of intention. While I completely acknowledge my own sets of *whys,* on a business and personal level, I also realize that over the years, as I design mainly for others, my *whys* can be so minute and insignificant when compared to some of the *whys* I have encountered through research and observation.

Asking *Why* is an invitation for reflection. Even identifying what the *whys* are requires presence, stillness, mindfulness, thoughtful consideration, and deep listening. Determining the answers to the *whys* can challenge and expand our problem-solving skills by requiring us to think differently, broaden our horizons, and become determined and innovative interior archaeologists.

Discovering the answers to the question *Why* can be extremely challenging. For some it is such a broad question that they spend their lifetime searching for it. Still, it is important to investigate and discern the answers to *"why,"* and especially the answers that make sense and feel right to one's head and heart in the "now." Once you perceive the answer, once you excavate the cornerstone of your intention, you are ready to imbue subsequent action with purpose and meaning. From this rich, solid, and nurturing base of intention, the rest of the questions follow:

• How do we execute?

- How do we make it work?

- Can we afford it?

- Can we postpone this?

- What can we gain today versus tomorrow?

The questions can continue on, ad infinitum.

Sample of *Whys* in Product Development

Why are we creating this?
Why would people care?
Why do people need this?
*Why would people want this and
pay, or not pay, for this?*
*Why isn't this product/service out
there already?*
Why us?
*Why does this product/service
matter now?*
*Why would people buy from
our competitors?*
Why is this product/service unique?

The Head and the Heart: The Beneficial Tension between Emotion and Reason

In our examination of the *why, how,* and *what* in this journey from the inside out, we are building a design argument for action and outcome that reflects both sensitivity and sensibility. In his treatise *Rhetorica,* Aristotle validated that the power of emotion was critical to influencing and motivating people.[31]

Seneca posited that reason ruled only if it was kept separate from emotion.[32] And eighteenth-century English philosopher George Campbell suggested that emotion and reason were allies that together compelled the assimilation of knowledge.[33] Emotion and reason have been dancing alongside one another since communication began, and while individually each has its strengths, a positive relationship between the two can be the most powerful tool of all for shaping behavior and attitude.

The Head

One way to construct a persuasive argument is to reveal facts in a logically based manner. The head is always thinking, analyzing, strategizing, comparing, adding, and subtracting. We elevate and trust in those rational processes. Consider our fascination with the Vulcans and their ability to suppress emotions, think, and act logically. Given our trend toward STEM education as a national priority in a global marketplace, do we aspire to a Vulcan mindset? Will science, technology, engineering, and mathematics be enough to evolve the human species to the next level? What would we gain? Efficiency? Scalability? Profitability? When the numbers indicate more or less, grow or scale back, amass or get rid of, or automate or create one-offs, a Vulcan, with cool computational indifference, could easily impose action and adjust design and behavior for the sake of the bottom line and optimal outcomes. Are we there yet? Do we want to be?

The Heart

Another method of crafting a persuasive argument is to appeal and respond to people's emotions. The heart is the seat of love, compassion, joy, empathy, sadness, anger, frustration, jealousy, and all the range of human emotion, both the good and the bad.

To possess emotional intelligence equips us to look beyond black and white. It enhances our ability to navigate sticky situations, resolve conflicts, know (in our heart) what is right or wrong and everything in between. The heart celebrates the human spirit and fuels our ability to hope, wonder, seek, aspire, experiment, try, fail, and succeed. Passion, gutsiness, and true grit make their home there. The human voice finds its expression there.

> The heart celebrates the human spirit and fuels our ability to hope, wonder, seek, aspire, experiment, try, fail, and succeed.

The fruits of the heart include connectivity, emotional attachment, love, passion, and memories that comfort and make you yearn for more. The heart is the premiere target of corporate advertisers. They know that if you can touch people's emotions, you are likely able to also get them, on impulse, to open their wallets. The heart, with all of its intuitive intelligence, is not always wise. Sometimes it needs a chaperone. The mind and heart work best when they work together.

Mind and Heart Coherence

The goal of any persuasive argument is to win. The methods are different. Taking the logical path is like taking the interstate with a data-driven decision that saves time. The emotion-based way of the heart is akin to taking the scenic route where you enjoy nature and beautiful scenery. To balance both, to know when and how to break the rules and set new rules, was the purpose of Dr. Spock in the popular *Star Trek* series.[34]

We've seen hundreds of movies out there where at some point the hero has to make tough choices that will either save or kill his family, friends, neighbors, and sometimes the world. There is always this tension around doing the "right" thing. Will the decision be made based on hard data or gut instincts, experience, and the heart?

When the heart and mind work together, they realize a state of coherence and create an experience of synergy. The outcome is greater harmony in addressing daily projects, communications and challenges. Achieving this state of coherence helps increase mental clarity and capacity for accurate discernment. For more than 20 years, the Institute of HeartMath (IHM), an internationally recognized, non-profit research and education organization, has been researching and advancing understanding of heart/brain interactions, heart rhythm coherence, and the physiology of optimal learning and performance. This leader in coherence-building techniques identifies the energetic heart as the access point for natural inner technology that elevates choices to a much higher level of effectiveness. Recognizing that heart/mind feelings are primary drivers for our biological systems and influence our behaviors and choices, IHM's technologies and programs help people consciously develop heart/mind coherence.[35]

The organization asserts that a feedback loop exists between all humans and the earth's energetic systems and that there is a relationship between earth's magnetic fields and collective human emotions, intentions and resonance. Research indicates that achieving and maintaining a state of coherence increases flow, effectiveness and the potential for higher outcomes, and benefits people, animals and the environment. Everyone contributes to the field, and heart coherence leads to greater social coherence, which means that if people became more mindful of and responsible for their thoughts and feelings, the world would be a better place. According to Doc Childre, the founder of HeartMath and consultant to business leaders, scientists, and educators, "As more of humanity practices heart-based living, it will qualify the 'rite of passage' into the next level of consciousness. Using our heart's intuitive guidance will become common sense based on practical intelligence."[36]

Synergy between mind and heart does not live simply in the personal sphere. It is a practice to be applied across all dimensions of life. In our living, working, and loving, the integration of mind and heart leads us to recognize and cultivate, in the most sincere way possible, true appreciation, trust, respect and love. It helps us stay aligned with our path and purpose, both in the short term with current projects, decisions, and actions, and in the long term as those "moments" accumulate to form and add tension and intention to our life path and purpose. And it helps us begin to understand what is of real value. We realize that we do not exist in a vacuum, and maybe we are something more than just a random collision of ideas and unusual suspects.

In Verne Harnish's book *Scaling Up*, the author reminds us of our humanity and potential for success as well as fallibility. Despite our technology, it's clear who really drives the action:

> *In the end, we're all in the same business: people to people. None of us sell to companies; we deal with the people (consumers) inside these companies, who have the same motivations, challenges, and emotions as any other person.*[37]

Creatives need to achieve that "coherence" between balancing data and creating with the heart, which is a common tension when it comes to innovating products, services and brand experiences. How often do we hear, "the data is showing us this; therefore, we need to do more of it." So many managers have their job performance tied to conversion rates. Imagine not getting your bonus because you didn't increase traffic to your company's website by a certain percentage. Or losing your job because of lack of "results." That kind of result/reward mentality only breeds managers solely focused on conversions and numbers, regardless of what those numbers signify. It is important to look at the broader picture, to have the entire story with which to work, and to not lose sight of the human element within all of it.

When we are conscious of that positive tension between mind and heart, and feel the balance it affords us, we can also then be mindful of being reflective and not reactive. I have worked with teams that would redo a brand's entire color palette just because two followers on Twitter mentioned how much they didn't like the new blue. The rationale is "Data is showing us that!" Well, here is another consideration. If your Twitter fan base is only 20% of your entire customer base, and only

> When we are conscious of that positive tension between mind and heart, and feel the balance it affords us, we also then can be mindful of being reflective and not reactive.

two out of 20% tweeted how much they hated the blue, is that enough justification to change the blue? There is action, reaction, and over-reaction. A better approach would be to review your intention around the project and then really look into that 20% and determine the percentage of actual users, actual customers, fans, trolls, fake accounts, etc. Some of us are so focused on hard data we forget to resurface, reacquaint ourselves with the breadth and dimension of the project, and stay open to fresh perspectives.

Qualitative data can be helpful. Oftentimes, clients come to me asking for a website redo. They furnish me with a list of goals: what they think the website should be, what they think customers want to see, and the list goes on and on. But when I do some user interviews, I discover that users are not using the website the way the brand thought. Data, it turns out, can be used and manipulated to win any argument, especially if we don't take the time to look beyond what appears to be the obvious in order to discover what is really happening.

Nurturing that balance between mind and heart helps cultivate mindfulness. It allows us to connect with that greater compassionate intelligence we know as consciousness. The more mindful we become, the more engaged we become in the creative process of the universe that gives our life true purpose and meaning.

Live Your Purpose

Many people feel they are here for a reason, although they may not be sure what their purpose or path in this life may be. The self-help industry today is thriving as people explore a multiplicity of methods and programs designed to help them unlock the mystery of themselves and discover their life's true purpose and how to make each day rewarding and meaningful.

For many, meaning and purpose are derived from the awareness that every effort results in a positive impact on someone else's life and contributes toward a collective good. We all admire people who seem to be doing great good in the world, and we particularly hearken to stories of people who overcome incredible odds and terrific challenge to realize a dream and pay it forward.

As children, we all have dreams of being something extraordinary: a doctor, a fireman, an explorer, a superhero. We latch onto icons and archetypes that inspire us, resonate with us at our core and cause us to drink from the river of inspiration. We have individuated, and we want to do more than survive: we want to be known. As we live and grow, we learn, we experience, we undergo conditioning, and we set goals. Ellen Petry Leanse, an Apple Pioneer, Google alum, teacher, author, entrepreneur, and advisor created a framework she calls an *Intention Map* that helps us think about our lives and goals and whether we are living according to our intention or living *in-tension*. Knowing life is a process, we constantly explore new possibilities and harness momentum to expand our potential. If we are mindful of our core intention, our journeying will seem less random. We will recognize roads to nowhere, turning points, and when the things we do are in alignment with our purpose.

A friend of mine, Tennyson Pinheiro, the author of *The Service Startup,* once said, "A designer's life is their toolbox." I agree wholeheartedly. The entirety of our life experience informs our work. Often it isn't until we actually stop and reflect on the path our life has taken us, and its seemingly arbitrary infusion of people, events, and challenges, that we recognize we have been navigating a course of purpose, though, granted, we may often feel lost at sea.

Mari Kuraishi, CEO and cofounder of one of the original crowdfunding platforms "GlobalGiving," often speaks about her evolution from being a young woman who was just interested in studying all things Russian and avoiding becoming an office lady (OL) in Japan to helping create literally a movement of philanthropy. Mari had a sense, at her core, of what she wanted for her life. She also had a profound sense of what she did not want and would not settle for. With the dissolution of the USSR, she saw all that she had schooled and trained for collapse in an instant. When the dust cloud settled in her new reality, other opportunities arose. Simply by staying true to herself and focusing on making decisions that made sense to her head and her heart in the NOW, Mari ultimately crafted a life that optimizes her ability to do incredible good in the world. This gives her a sense of fulfillment and happiness every day.

Our lives are the toolbox from which we craft and create the reality around us. Mari believes her life experiences were instrumental in helping her put her organization together. She cannot say if she is living her life purpose. She is much more comfortable feeling she is living whatever her purpose is in this present moment. If you do the best you can in the NOW, Mari feels you start opening up "levels" that weren't accessible to you before.

Mari didn't map out a life of entrepreneurship or leadership for herself. She feels that by not having grandiose expectations from the outset helped maintain her peace of mind. She never berated herself for not meeting her expectations. Instead, she simply sensed her expectations growing as her capabilities increased. Her careful crafting of a unique business model, where the different customer segments served reinforce each other, were key to her organization's success. Mari likens it to a slow evolutionary process where small changes that were advantageous were kept, and the changes that weren't helpful were jettisoned.

The value for creating GlobalGiving is that Mari gets to surround herself with amazing people who feel as passionately as she does about what can be done when obstacles are removed and resources conveyed to amazing people in every community in the world.[38] GlobalGiving has four guiding principles/values:

1. Being always open to the power of good ideas

2. Continually experimenting and constantly listening, acting, learning and repeating

3. Never settling and recognizing the responsibility of questioning the "rules"

4. Being committed to acting promptly, enthusiastically and professionally so that others are wowed by the interaction

These guidelines are critical in helping everyone in the organization know what to do in any given situation, and Mari believes these are the values she brought to the venture.

As I reflect on Mari's story, and the stories of all the people who encourage and inspire me, I realize that lives lived with wisdom and purpose, lives lived mindfully, with a balance of mind and heart, are lives that provide positive impact and contribute to the greater good. These are people who lead by example and show us the *what* and *how* of being a better human. As creatives, we don't just live our lives and pursue the passion of our profession so that we can tell our story. We do what we do so that we can help others tell their story.

A Gift of Our Story

"I really appreciated your story and I am so grateful to you for sharing it with me. I feel there is a universal story—and it's always the same. It's about a person—someone like you and me—waking up one day and saying, 'I want something more. I believe I can do something meaningful/important/different. But I must move—go somewhere I've never been before to realize this potential, to fill this hunger.'

And so we go to a new place. And we work hard. And we eat bitterness and endure sleeplessness, hunger and discouragement, performing with no net, hanging on tightly to our vision of something more. Every single day trying to decide what to keep from our old life and what to abandon. Making painful choices. Making a way out of no way at all. Then success. Then the question of how much of my story do I want to tell and to whom. Because it is a precious story of building a life out of one's own imagination. And the wisdom that comes from struggle. We don't want anyone learning the wrong lessons, or making the wrong assumptions. Our story is our own personal treasure and it is the one thing we don't owe the world. We choose when and how we make a gift of our story and our wisdom."

—Angela Blanchard, CEO of BakerRipley, commenting on Mel Lim sharing her personal story on adversities, failures, and ambition.

Questions to Ask When Designing Technology Experiences

The Whos

- To whom are we telling this story?

  Investors?

  Partners?

  Media?

  Public?

  Customers?

  Industry Experts?

  Competitors?

- Who will maintain and update the company's story?

The Whys

- Why would your customers care?

- Why are we telling this story? And why tell this story now?

- Is it to prove that the tech company is the leader in its space?

- Is it to demo that the product is freaking awesome and might even achieve world peace?

- Is it to raise money?

- Is it to squash the noise of industry competitors?

The Whats

- *What* covers a lot of ground, from concept to launch, and all the planning in between:

  What is the content?

  What are the metrics for success?

  What are we measuring against?

  What is the company's goal?

  What is the competitive market like?

  What is the budget?

Add your own questions here:

_____   _____   _____

_____   _____   _____

_____   _____   _____

_____   _____   _____

_____   _____   _____

The Whens

- When is this story being told:

    When the product is ready to launch?

    When SEs (sales engineers) do their pitches/demos?

    When CFOs or CIOs do their pitches to some large organization?

The Hows

- How are you telling it?

    Is it being delivered in person?

    Will a PPT be used?

    Do you intend to communicate it through a video animation?

    Are you distributing it via social media channels?

    Do you envision Cirque du Soleil troops flying around while you belt out your company's 30-second elevator pitch?

The Wheres

- Where is the company heading?

- Where is the technology taking us?

- Where will this technology be two, five, or ten years from now?

- Where will our competitors be two, five, or ten years from now?

- Where will this content live, and for how long?

_____

_____

_____

_____

_____

_____

_____

_____

_____

_____

_____

_____

_____

_____

_____

Summary:
Wisdom + Passion = Purpose

As craftspeople, we recognize that our passion for our work is buried deep inside of us. We generously allocate time for creating and often make personal sacrifices to do so. It's important to balance our love of creating with wisdom and purpose so we don't lose sight of our goals and priorities. We must know who we are, and why we do what we do. The question *Why* is the main driver of all action. It frames the issue and approach, helps us set our intentions, and invites reflection. It then radiates out to *How* and finally *What* it is we do. Expression of our craft comes from the heart. In examining why, how, and what, we balance mind and heart and build a sensitive and sensible design argument for action and outcome.

The gifts of the mind include thinking, analyzing, strategizing, comparing, adding and subtracting. The heart focuses on connectivity, emotional attachment, love, passion, and compassion. Corporate advertisers target the heart. When mind and heart work together they create an experience of synergy and a state of coherence which increases flow, effectiveness, potential for higher outcomes, and benefits for people, animals and the environment. Synergy between the two impacts all dimensions of life and keeps us aligned with our path and purpose. Coherence guards against the result/reward mentality in business, where managers focus solely on conversions and numbers.

Nurturing the balance between mind and heart helps cultivate mindfulness and the compassionate intelligence known as consciousness. Many people have a conscious awareness that they are here for a reason. The self-help industry brims with methods and programs designed to help people discover their purpose and live with intention. Mindful journeying limits excursions down random roads to nowhere, and helps harness momentum so people can expand their potential.

As creatives, the entirety of our life experience informs our work. I take great inspiration from meeting remarkable people and learning their stories of struggle and success. I gravitate toward people who know who they are at their core, know what they want, who live in the NOW and who care to positively impact the world and contribute to the greater good. One such person is Mari Kuraishi, CEO and cofounder of one of the original crowdfunding platforms, GlobalGiving. Her organization follows four guiding principles:

1. Be open to the power of good ideas

2. Continually experiment, listen, act, learn and repeat

3. Never settle, and recognize the responsibility of questioning the "rules"

4. Act promptly, enthusiastically and professionally

Through Mari's example and the inspiring examples of other creative people, I realize that we don't just live our lives and pursue the passion of our profession so that we can tell our story. We do what we do so that we can help others tell their story. The stories we share about our successes and struggles on our way to discovering our path and our purpose then become the gifts of inspiration that we give one another.

6 Creative Guru 101: Learn to Be Mindful, Accountable, and Trustworthy

Ideation and Creativity

"We are what we think.
All that we are arises with our thoughts.
With our thoughts, we make our world."

—Buddha

Creativity comes from within. Our thoughts, ideas, and actions originate with us. We are the source of all that we think, do, and bring into this world. And as the source of all that we create, we must be ready and willing to follow up with what we birth into being, and take credit or blame for it. To not be bound by a sense of accountability, care, or conscience around what we have manifested, and to be steadily moving on to the next conquest or experience without once looking back is not only neglectful and unethical, it is problematic and disruptive.

To be disconnected and indifferent toward the fruits of our ideation reflects a lack of conscientiousness that feels decidedly uncraftsman-like. Not standing behind our ideas, our work, and the fruits of our labor points to a (growing) creative disorder. Our accelerated world, with all its impulsivity and clamoring after the next best thing, only enables and encourages this lack of connection to our creative efforts. We must refine our ethical sensibilities and create passionately and responsibly, with complete follow-through.

Cultivate the Beginner's Mind

"In the beginner's mind there are many possibilities, in the expert's mind there are few."

—Shunryu Suzuki

Let's begin at the beginning, with something we call "beginner's mind." Here we set the stage for the inception of ideas, knowing that creativity is a gestation, birth, and parenting process. By being fully engaged at the start with each project, we help ensure our ongoing involvement and commitment with our work, from evolution to maturity.

In order to be a master, we must first be a student. And as a student, we must be open, teachable, and willing to set aside all preconceived ideas, notions, and ways of doing things so that new awareness can be planted, take root, and eventually come to fruition. This ability to be the fertile field for new growth is what is known in Zen Buddhism as Shōshin (初心), a concept that means "beginner's mind." In the state of beginner's mind, we are fresh and open to the broadest range of possibilities in every moment. We are in that state of "not knowing," with no expectation or judgment, so we cannot anticipate outcomes. Rather, there is potential in the eternal present, for joy, adventure, excitement, and fulfillment. Anticipation of what is coming, what will be, keeps us focused wholly in the present, and full of wonder and appreciation.

How does one cultivate a beginner's mind, a mind that is open and awake to new experience, or an entirely different view of an existing situation? The personal physician to His Holiness the Dalai Lama says, "Empty your bowl of yesterday's rice."[39] Taste life anew and try living each moment with a sense of wonder. The beginner's mind is a mind that is free to wander and revel, without interference from the "expert mind" where the ego gets bossy and defensive.

Beginner's mind is possible when one is in a state of mindfulness. Mindfulness is the practice of awareness that life, with all its wonders, exists in the here and now. In mindfulness, one consciously directs their awareness to experience in the present moment. Thich Nhat Hanh, a renowned Zen master, poet, and writer of more than 40 books says that the energy of mindfulness contains the energy of concentration.[40] When your mindfulness is powerful, your concentration is also powerful, and you can achieve breakthroughs of great insight and understanding about anything on which you are meditating. Not being present and not being mindful puts us in the opposite state: distracted and forgetful. According to Thich Nhat Hanh, most people operate in a state of forgetfulness, caught up in their cares, worries, and fears, and all the many things they have going on at any given time.[41] Studies have shown that all our many distractions impede our comprehension of things we would choose to learn or make decisions around. In fact, several studies have shown that reading text punctuated with links causes weaker comprehension than reading plain text. In 2007, a study involving 100 participants shown a multimedia presentation of pictures, sounds and words suggested lower comprehension levels than if they would have simply read plain text.[42] Distractions prevent us from being fully present and living our life deeply, or mindfully plying our craft with laser focus.

When we are in an authentic state of mindfulness, we are silent. Verbal and mental chatter cease. Our entire being feels the refreshment of "quietness." It is similar to when farmers allow their fields to lie fallow so that the soil can replenish its nutrients naturally and once again become fertile and ready for planting. Mindfulness reboots our mental processes, stimulates creativity, sharpens perceptions, heightens sensory acuity, and facilitates better decision making. It is the creative's "mental detox" where we detach, de-stress, and allow ourselves to simply be in that magical moment of fresh beginning where insight is birthed.

The ideation process requires time for reflection and simmering so that there can be an unimpeded flow of ideas and new possibilities. Researchers from INSEAD, one of the world's largest graduate business schools, and the University of Pennsylvania's Wharton Business School found that meditation and mindfulness were instrumental in lifting moods and shifting mental bias around both past events and future outcomes to achieve a fresh and uncluttered focus on decisions in the NOW.[43] Mindfulness, it seems, has a way of making all things new.

Why, you ask, am I telling you about beginner's mind and mindfulness when you thought you were reading a book on taking the time to craft your projects in a high-velocity world? We live in a global world, where cultures have been brought together to share their ideas, histories, traditions, and age-old practices. What a remarkable time this is in the evolution of our world and our species. We have almost instant access to knowledge and practices that have been cultivated over centuries and are just now being shared. As discerning creatives and craftspeople, we have the opportunity to fill our "toolbox" with time-tested and proven teachings from traditions all over the world that align with our intention to master our art and craft real value.

Truth: The Stamp of Authenticity

A variation on the kanji (Japanese character writing) of the term "beginner's mind" offers a related term, Shōshin (正真), which means "correct truth." It is used to denote a genuine signature on artwork, or refer to any person or thing that is authentic. As creatives, we care for our work to be authentic, wholly from us, to reflect our best skill and craftsmanship, and embody truth in form and function. In order to achieve truth in craftsmanship, an artist must allocate time to explore, experiment, and engage all the senses.

There must be a quiet space for reaching deeply within and finding the thought that would be form. Walt Whitman once said, "All truths wait in all things. They neither hasten their own delivery nor resist it."[44] We must wait for that voice. For that "Song of Ourselves." This indulgence triggers discoveries, facilitates new connections, enhances learning, distills understanding, and hones craft. For many of us, the training and practice of going within to discover what is there, to find our truth, and then decide how to express it in the world began with childhood music lessons.

For example, my own experience with playing musical instruments as a child contributed greatly to my development in a number of different areas. I never liked playing the organ. It was passed down from my aunt to my sister who refused it and chose the piano. So I was stuck with this old 1970s Yamaha Electone organ. Regardless of how poor we were, my parents insisted that we each master one musical instrument. I ended up learning to play the recorder/flute, the organ, the melodica, and I sang. Looking back over my 10 years of lessons, medals, and endless practice, I realized how my music activities shaped my approach to problem solving. First off, it made me ambidextrous. On days when I needed to be at my fullest allegro, my left hand would be drawing

with a Wacom pen, and my right with the mouse. It also made me both a creative and analytical thinker, sharpened my math skills, and contributed to my becoming an artist. Music, it turns out, has this transformative effect on people who pursue it.

Over the last five years, I've had the pleasure to work with David Gibson, the CMO of Varonis. I find him to be one of the most creative, thoughtful, and strategic leaders with whom I've had the pleasure of working. In his approach to projects, he is generally composed, very open to feedback and ideas, and able to apply original thinking while working within a constrictive yet well-defined framework of budgets, deadlines, and limited resources. He also knows when to push boundaries, exceed limitations, and drive his team to think bigger, better, faster and smarter, while keeping them aligned and focused. It turns out that David is also a musician at heart. Music taught him several key lessons, all of which are measures of authentic investment in and execution of craft:

Lesson 1: Humility

David remembered being interested in music from an early age. He loved to sing. His Mom recorded him when he was four or five singing along to the Monkees' song "The Last Train to Clarksville." He remembered how shocked he was to hear himself for the first time and how different the recording was from how he thought he sounded. He asked, "Do I really sound like that?" "Yes," answered his mother enthusiastically, not realizing he felt horrified.

Music taught David the importance of listening to and watching recordings/videos of himself. He considers it profoundly instructive because it also taught him to observe the delivery of his speech and thoughts. He also learned to accept that improving was a process—sometimes a very long process. Humility, it turns out, is the conscience of all endeavor.

Lesson 2: Practice Makes Things Possible and Sometimes Perfect

Different instruments help one challenge their skills and abilities and express their creative voice in distinctive and diverse ways. David plays several instruments. He reflected on his thought processes/mental noise while learning to master each one. It sounded like this: That can't be right. There's no way I can do that quickly enough or with enough control to play in rhythm, at the right volume, and with a nice tone. And I certainly won't be able to do it twice or more in a row. One such moment occurred as he played chords on the guitar. He recalled that the first time he made a D chord, he had to place each finger of his left hand one at a time on the strings with his right hand, and then do the same thing when he made a G chord. It took him 60 seconds to form each chord and he couldn't fathom how he could possibly go back and forth between those two chords in less than a second.

David learned early in life how amazing and malleable our brains are and how quickly they adapt. He discovered that through regular and consistent practice, sometimes over a long period of time, he could do things he once considered beyond his ability, whether it was playing chords quickly, playing something different with his left hand than his right on the piano, or even juggling. And he learned how rewarding it felt to know his skills were improving. According to Dr. Norman Doidge, the author of *The New York Times* best sellers *The Brain That Changes Itself* and *The Brain's Way of Healing,* the brain can indeed change. The brain possesses neuroplasticity, the ability to rewire itself through mental experience. Doidge explains, "one of the core laws of neuroplasticity is that neurons that fire together wire together, meaning that repeated mental experience leads to structural changes in the brain neurons that process that experience."[45] Through neuroplasticity, the brain can reform and adjust itself to respond to new situations, injuries, and diseases. In David's case, his immersion in music and the practice of playing instruments developed his musical abilities and gave him lifelong skills he could then apply to all areas of his life.

Lesson 3: Patience

Music reminded David to be humble, to practice and to make friends with patience. He learned to play over and over again. Sometimes he felt like his performance was consistently mediocre. Then he would realize he'd gotten better. And then he'd seem to backslide to mediocre again. Eventually it stopped mattering to him where his performance fell on any particular day. Instead he focused on the momentum and the experience of the journey.

Lesson 4: Focus

Focus can mean the difference between really doing something well and not doing it properly at all. If you're thinking about something else, you're not fully present and engaged with your activity, and therefore you're either not doing it right, or certainly not doing it to the best of your ability. Practicing music taught David that his determination to play required an investment of time and attention. He needed to practice mindfully rather than just go through the motions, and he needed to listen actively.

As in any activity, sometimes we need to break our focus and shift our attention in order to decompress and give our brains a chance to reboot. Our brains crave variety, so there is always temptation to roam. Sometimes it is in the best interest of our practice if we allow our minds to shift to a related task. That way, we get a mental refresh, but we don't lose sight of the whole. We learn that everything we do must be somehow in service to that project upon which we are most focused.

Lesson 5: Passion and Flow

Attending music school taught David that he was not meant to be a professional musician. In order to play professionally, music must be your life. It is all-consuming and requires that you quickly abandon other interests. Music must be the only thing you think about. David was self-aware enough to know he had other interests, and that music was more of an avocation or hobby, something to bring him joy and inspiration as he pursued his career path.

Through music, and playing in the pre-college symphony at Julliard, David never lost his sense of awe at how seemingly disparate elements of "noise" can be brought together to form harmony. Within the magic of a symphony, one can experience community resonance. What begins as a cacophony of noise transforms into a symphony of harmonious sound. As the musicians, passionate about their vocation, extend themselves into the integrative experience, they enjoy a pleasurable and satisfying process. One can almost drift away in the resultant endorphin rush, and the musicians find themselves completely immersed in "flow," an optimal state of complete absorption and suspended self-consciousness, where time and space seem to not exist. The flow state is an ideal and intrinsically rewarding meditative state that can foster a sense of happiness, meaning and accomplishment across the landscape of all positive work and creative endeavor.

Imposter Syndrome:
Zero Calories in Humble Pie

We creatives relish the pure, organic truth of the work that we do. As we go about busily focused on every excruciating detail, humbly working our craft and sharing it with the world, we sometimes cringe when others refer to us as "experts" in our industry. Where is the Shōshin (正) in that, we wonder? Oddly, some of the most successful people experience something known as the Imposter Syndrome. It is hard to be referred to as an expert when we see ourselves as earnest students constantly immersed in new learnings and exploration. The title "expert" seems to refer to someone who has already "arrived," who has ascended the mountaintop and no longer needs to strive, struggle, and reach for the next delicate iteration or startling perspective.

In an article in *Psychology Today,* Dr. Matthew Lieberman identified this dilemma (which he calls the "paradox of expertise") as akin to being caught in a vice.[46] He said that at some point in our development, we move from being learners to knowers, and the better we are at learning, the worse this problem can become. When either we or someone else labels us an expert, it becomes hard to put that identity aside and once again become a learner. We're ashamed of having to let others know that we don't know all they feel confident we know.[47] The key is to stay humble and honest with ourselves and others, and to know the truth of our trajectory. I know that being called an expert sometimes makes me feel as though I have stopped learning and am no longer open to the beginner's mindset of many possibilities, the 10,000 ways of doing things. But I never forget my roots. I know that fluency begets fluidity, and I get a rush off the wonder I feel when the light bulbs upstairs switch on.

Accountability:
A Measure of Creative Integrity

Knowing and valuing the truth of our work doesn't just require us to stay humble around the success of our process and product. It also demands that we hold ourselves accountable for the outcome and experience. There is no quick way to producing craft. The creative process takes time. Owning something involves birthing, shaping with your hands, creating something out of nothing. Producing something inspired by the union of your heart and brain, and making that idea tangible and shareable is a very personal experience. In order for anyone to experience true accountability, they must first risk producing something, be it a good or bad idea. They must risk an experience of failure.

Fail to Succeed

On June 7, 2017, innovation researcher Samuel West debuted a museum exhibition in Helsingbord, Sweden. The exhibition studies creativity from an innovative perspective. It showcases failure as an inextricable part of the creative process. Failure must be a part of the process, and by this I mean failure in the sense of many versions, many prototypes, and where time could have been spent to rediscover better, faster, more efficient ways of doing things. *Financial Times* columnist Tim Harford wrote in his book *Adapt: Why Success Always Starts with Failure* that we must be prepared to fail productively.[48]

It is important to admit we have erred, to not get too attached to our plan, to keep our emotions and especially ego out of it, to create a safe space to fail, and to try many new ideas while weeding out the ones that don't work. Progressive companies realize that "great success depends on great risk, and failure is simply a common by product."[45] There is room for error and accountability is encouraged. Leaders proactively deflect issues, thinking is more fearless, creative and strategic, confidence soars, and companies generate higher revenue.

I admit to having failed in creative pursuits. My fizzling firsthand experiences taught me so many important lessons. In 2003, at 26 years of age, I started my own company, JOY by Mel Lim, with an initial product line of handcrafted greeting cards. In 2005 I launched that product line and in the space of one year was selling in more than 500 stores, and had more than 1,000 media features nationally and internationally, including London, UAE and Tokyo. My business expanded to home décor items as well. In 2008, the recession took its toll on JOY, and I had to recognize it was time to let go and move on to my next iteration of entrepreneurship. Business and craftsmanship are always personal. While JOY was not a "mistake" on my part per se, but rather a victim of economic times, it was a great teacher on the importance of being nimble, flexible, resilient, smart, and optimistic.

Flexibility and a willingness to look at your project or business in a new way can be key to taking it from failure to success. For example, Earl Tupper of Tupperware fame had a showroom on Fifth Avenue and lots of advertising, but still was not doing well financially. Brownie Wise, who worked for a company called Party Plan, began selling Tupperware at in-home parties. The concept took off. In a post-war era, women could meet neighbors, maintain their domestic responsibilities, and make their own money. In 1951, Tupper took his product out of retail stores and sold them at parties. He made Brownie Wise the first Vice President of the home parties business.[49] Tupper was so successful, he sold his company for $16 million in 1957 to Rexall Drugs.

Considering that nearly eight out of ten businesses fail in the first 18 months, you would think there would be a culture for learning through risking and failing.[50] Well, actually, there is an annual private conference titled *FailCon,* created by Cass Phillipps, who survived a failed startup, that gathers technology entrepreneurs, investors, developers, and designers to study their own and others' failures and prepare for success. Failure should not be a dirty little secret that is swept under the rug.[51] It's better to dispense with ego and hubris, really talk, share perspectives and war stories, and be smarter and more

> Failure should not be a dirty little secret that is swept under the rug.

prepared for what's ahead. And sometimes we have to do that thing we least want to: we have to pull the plug on a project and not chase after our losses or try to convince ourselves that a mistake doesn't matter.

In our competitive global market we increasingly feel the tension between efficiency and automation versus devotion to craft and taking time to ponder and think. There must be a balance of both. It is important for us to continually practice and hone our basic, hands-on skills and stimulate our cognitive abilities. Too much dependency on automation and technology leaves us disconnected and even helpless to do anything if we cannot call on all of our innate tools to take over when circumstances dictate. Following a series of pilot-error airline crashes, NASA research psychologist Steve Casner conducted a study of the impact of cockpit technology on a pilot's ability to fly a plane without the use of automation.[52] The results found that most pilots had rusty stick-and-rudder skills and their ability to think through situations was greatly compromised:

> *However, when our pilots were asked to interpret something out of the ordinary, mentally keep track of where they were, and understand how and why the automation works, their performance quickly slumped. Four of our 16 pilots failed to keep track of their position and missed the airport altogether. Eight of 16 pilots placed the airplane in a near-stall condition four times or more before figuring out that their airspeed indicator had become unreliable.*[53]

The overuse and overdependence on technology is causing our cognitive skills to recede and making our ability to express ideas through hands-on processes awkward and foreign. As creatives, we must be able to master our craft and make sound, innovative choices and decisions that best serve our client, and our skills must be innate, fluid, and articulate.

When we are distanced from a hands-on connection with what we create, our passion for it, our familiarity with and appreciation of every aspect and detail of it, suffers. Such arms-length, sensory-deprived "interaction" with our creations can result in the production of short-term junk and increased unwillingness to accept responsibility for outcomes. Without hands-on interaction comes distance, and with distance comes anonymity. Who crashed the plane? The pilot or the failed systems? Ultimately what goes south in this scenario? TRUST!

> **Accountability means putting our word and reputation on the line. Someone is counting on us—and we should care that someone is counting on us. If failure's not an option, that can feel like too much of responsibility—or a liability—to take on.** [54]
>
> —Deborah Mills-Scofield, Mentor, Entrepreneur, Investor

The Holy Grail of Relationships: Trust

Trust between clients and creatives is developed through connection. Clients like to know that the people they have retained to look after their interests and bring their projects to life are deeply connected to their work at every level, are mindfully attuned to the process, and are dedicated to delivering a quality product and realizing success for everyone involved. Trust grows as clients and creatives communicate and feel secure enough to reveal vulnerabilities, hopes, aspirations, and desire for growth and improvement. And trust increases when creatives take responsibility for what they produce.

There are three key ways that owning one's work and mistakes can create a "relationship of trust" and make a person more respected, esteemed, and successful in the long run:

- Accountability demonstrates responsibility

- Honesty shows integrity

- Being upfront reveals relatability

This "relationship" of trust comes full circle. It informs our craft. Our clients find peace of mind working with trusted professionals, and consequently we work even harder to maintain that trust.

Where Rapid Prototyping Reigns, Trust Wanes

"When it is obvious that the goals cannot be reached, don't adjust the goals, adjust the action steps."

—Confucius

So how does that new game in town, rapid prototyping, impact the important prongs of the client/creative relationship, especially since it was introduced in the interest of expediting deliverables in a competitive environment? With its "quick artist" process of generating sketch after sketch, ideas are rapidly and cheaply generated in order to test the market and gain traction. Business now uses this methodology at scale; i.e., design thinking, lean startups, jugaad, and agile. These processes reduce time and research and development costs, but don't necessarily translate into valid solutions with any longevity.

Recently, Ogi Kavazovic, CMO and SVP Product Strategy at Flatiron Health, delivered a poignant article on *First Round Review,* about rethinking Agile at Enterprise Startups.[55] Kavazovic noted that a lack of understanding about whatever is being designed for either B2B or B2C by using the same playbook can seriously and detrimentally impact both product development and sales and marketing. He suggests that it is the antithesis of commitment to any long-term product goals, which affects the ability of sales and business teams to close any long-term deals or key partnerships.[56]

In agile design environments, creatives move quickly on to their next projects without opportunity to engage and reflect on their work. The pace discourages accountability for unsuccessful prototypes, or revising/reworking for real viability. When projects fail, or clients grow frustrated from a lack of interest in revising/reworking to make things right, trust implodes.

I question the wisdom of making rapid prototyping a normal operating procedure. At some point we're going to want to bring the next *Mona Lisa*, *Falling Water*, or Taj Mahal into the world. We must slow things down and remember to reflect and consider. It's important to review the product of our efforts and ask ourselves what we have birthed into being. What has the execution of our creative sensibilities brought into our environment? Have we been fully engaged (active and reflective) in our design process? Are our projects the embodiment of our best effort? Do we stand by what we create? Do we have trust and fluency with our own skills? Have we earned and won the trust of the populations for and with whom we work and create? What do our efforts say about us?

Understanding who your users are versus your actual buyers is a crucial distinction when it comes to designing products. Yes, we've all heard it: place users first. If there are no users, there is no business. Design for people. Of course user research is crucial to the development of any products/services, but understanding market dynamics as a whole is equally important. Your competition, global trends, regulations, and other influences are all important factors that would impact a buyer's decision.

In Kavazovic's experience, the pitfalls of an agile design process as noted above boil down to a key misunderstanding: agile development and longer-term planning are NOT the mutually exclusive modus operandi the tech world has portrayed them to be. He makes the following import delineation and suggestion:

Agile is really good for making sure that you create a successful user experience. But it's important to separate that from the overall product roadmap, which requires meeting the needs of your buyer. The key is to take a two-pronged approach: 1) articulate a long-term product vision, but 2) establish a culture of flexibility when it comes to the details.[53]

I am a big proponent of ideation, the reiterative process, the constant yearning for improving an idea, and striving to make it better and better. After viewing the film *Jiro Dreams of Sushi,* I felt driven to write this book. Master Jiro inspires me toward constant improvement and the craftsmanship that comes with an unwavering commitment toward perfecting every detail of one's daily "art." Master Jiro does not give his customers (who wait six months to enjoy his culinary performance and pay an average of USD $300 per platter) "sketches." They purchase an "excellent, crafted experience" that is NOT a prototype. It's a piece of art.

Ready, Set...Product Debt

Having worked with startups in the software space in the past decade, I've seen companies struggle with shipping products, especially when they are bound by limited resources (time, money, and people), and demanding business goals. Creatives today are propelled by the mantra of "ship fast, fail fast, and reiterate." I found this reiterative process to be useful when developing a minimum viable product (MVP).

But as we progress in the product cycles, we start to accumulate technical and product debts stemming from half-baked coding. This culminates into procrastination around rectifying previously written codes, and delayed production of the "right" solutions or a more "polished" version of the product due to time and budgetary constraints. Kip Mitchell from Axure, a rapid prototyping enterprise software solutions company, defines *product debt* as "any aspect of a company's product which it knows is less complete, consistent, or polished than it could be, but which is released 'as is' anyway because the product has to get out the door."[57] Let's be clear. Adding icing onto a half-baked cake doesn't make it good. Ignoring or masking imperfections in any creative endeavor promotes a culture of mediocrity. The result is nothing more than creative pollution.

Keeping Creative Integrity Intact

Now let's look at the opposite approach and examine what we gain and lose when we really commit to delivering crafted experiences that we stand behind. And let's explore if there can be a balance of both efficiency and our art. We are always juggling requests, tasks, and choosing best methods to approach our work. We can think of these as rubber and glass balls. What do we identify as being absolute priority (glass balls), and what do we identify as being less crucial (rubber balls). If you drop a rubber ball, it just bounces around until you pick it up again. If you drop a glass ball, it shatters, and the damage is irreversible. Quality, reputation, and trust, all qualify as glass balls.

In the previous chapter, I mentioned how I had essentially dropped the crystal ball when my second boy was born, choosing my work commitment over my commitment as a new mom. Our real-world and personal experiences, if we are paying attention and being mindful, inform and help shape even our approaches to business and project management. In a recent *TIME* magazine article, business executives shared how fatherhood had impacted their style and acumen as CEOs, including their ability to exercise greater patience, to vary their management techniques, and to embrace risks.[58] I now approach every project with two steps.

First, I review my companies' core values, manifestos and missions to ensure continued alignment with the belief systems that guide my work. Second, I reflect on these important questions:

- If my dedication to quality is central to my success, what is it that I have to give up, given the available amount of time, budget, and human resources?

- What are the rubber balls, what are the glass balls, and how do I move forward without requiring a broom and dustpan?

- What can I do to ensure that that the project is successful, serves its purpose, and is something of which I can be proud?

- When, in the course of the project, is it beneficial and most efficient to use rapid prototyping as a way to explore, visualize, discuss, and test design options?

This book seeks to encourage those who create to reflect on what they are doing, how they are doing it, why, and what the results signify. As artists, we naturally swim in an almost etheric miasma of "aspiration soup." We pull our ideas from dreams and inspiration, and then strive to make them tangible and of service. In Chiang Mai, Thailand, there is a large Buddhist Temple with a lovely walking garden that has trees bearing signs containing Buddhist quotes for reflection. One quote says, "If everything is gotten dreamily, it will go away dreamily too."[59] It is a call to action for us to awaken and be thoughtful and earnest about our work and our craft. We have not only the ability, but also the duty to take responsibility for what we express on this earth in the hopes of contributing to the beauty of the world, and to assess the results of our actions. As Buckminster Fuller once said, "Total accountability and total feedback constitute the minimum and only perpetual motion system."[60] In other words, the quality of our lives, of ALL life, depends on the quality and integrity of our action. Will we take the time to mindfully consider our craft knowing that we are contributing, at a universal level, a process that will be either regenerative or degenerative, depending on the honesty and exquisiteness of our impulses? Perhaps it's time to unleash our inner turtle.

Case Study: Aaron Fulkerson, CEO of MindTouch

Our mind is the tool that helps determine our greatest possible outcomes. How we nurture it, open it, discipline it, and apply it will impact its ability to guide us in realizing our true purpose and achieving our fullest potential. Aaron Fulkerson, cofounder and CEO of San Diego-based MindTouch, a customer success-driven SaaS company, has been a lifelong champion and practitioner of investing in the mind to maximize potential. His personal story is a testimony to the concept of "beginner's mind." In fact, his company's website puts the philosophy front and center with a quote by Shunryu Suzuki, "In the beginner's mind, there are many possibilities, but in the expert's mind, there are few."

Aaron's journey began in Northern California's Morgan Hill farm country. The diversity of the region, with its large Asian population, helped shape Aaron's own philosophical approach to life. A Japanese friend introduced him to Buddhism. When visiting at his friend's house, he was shown old, leather-bound Dharma texts.

He learned about the Zen concept of Shōshin or beginner's mind, where one maintains an attitude of eager openness in the study of any subject. He understood Zanshin, which suggests a state of total awareness and the mental and physical readiness to react to any situation. And Kaizen, a Japanese word meaning "change for better," and which eventually evolved to mean a daily process for "continual improvement," also seeped into Aaron's personal and professional philosophy.

After barely graduating high school, Aaron spent several years backpacking around the United States and Europe, meeting new people, working odd jobs, and embracing new experiences. Driven to invest in the development of his own mind, he created a pattern of teaching himself by opting for new and unusual experiences, and indulging his insatiable thirst for reading. Aaron had begun crafting the life he'd been gifted. He approached each new undertaking with a profound sense of *Arete* (*Greek: ἀρετή*), a Greek word connoting excellence and living up to one's highest potential.

Aaron met his wife in Minnesota. He did some non-profit work, saw a need for people to connect online, began attending community college at age 25, and graduated from Chapel Hill at age 30. While in college with acutely astute peers, Aaron experienced feeling the imposter syndrome. He marveled how he, an older student, and the son of parents who were high school dropouts, could even be attending college. Later he would come to understand that self-doubt is the nature of the entrepreneur and it's important to be insanely optimistic.

In 2006, Aaron co-founded MindTouch. While it originally began as an open source project, the company navigated a degree of failure until it was able to see clearly how to succeed. It had tried serving too broad a market, so instead it developed a niche product for a specific market. Eventual success required a beginner's mind and crafting, focusing on the process, concentrating on every step, and determining what they could do better than anyone else. MindTouch evolved necessarily into a company that converts user manuals into a digital experience so that businesses can sell more product. The guiding principles at MindTouch are the Buddhist concepts of Shōshin, Zanshin and Kaizen. Aaron had Samurai art carved into the pillars in the breakroom to remind employees of these principles. And *Arete* (*Greek:* ἀρετή) is a core value at MindTouch.

Aaron shuns entitlement. He values honor and grit over privilege. In hiring for MindTouch, he looks for people who have overcome challenge and adversity and who have interesting stories. He finds that people who approach life and business with a beginner's mind are fun to be around because they live in the moment and see things as they are, not necessarily how things are going to be. There's less optimization and certainty, and more of a focus on lifelong learning. Aaron prefers to hire people who align with the company's values and are a good fit for the company's collaborative culture. As he says, he doesn't want to work with douche bags.

As much of a teacher as he is a CEO, Aaron urges his employees to immerse themselves in the beginner's mind process. He likes to deconstruct that process, which his salespeople find especially challenging as they tend to be numbers driven. The MindTouch business model places customers first. The employee teams are referred to as Success Teams. They work on Success Plans for MindTouch clients and their customers. Client success is everyone's focus as opposed to client happiness. That is another story. Happiness evolves. It cannot be pursued. A focus on success sometimes requires initial hardship as growth can be painful and uncomfortable, but a client's patience typically pays off. Their success, in turn, gives meaning and purpose to each MindTouch employee's client-focused effort.

Extremely mindful about his employees' well-being, Aaron takes a personal interest in each one of his 80+ workers. He knows that while he expects them to care about his clients' success, it is equally as important for his people to feel cared about in return and to have what they need to develop to their highest potential. He gave an employee with cancer three months of paid time off. An employee with post-partum depression received two months of PTO. Aaron encouraged another who'd found a dream job at Apple to take the job offer. Aaron is as invested in each team member's personal growth and success as he wants them to be with their clients' success.

In keeping with the philosophy of beginner's mind and having the awareness and readiness to react to any situation, MindTouch has evolved from being a company that never raised external cash in its first 10 years, to a company that in early 2016 raised a modest $12 million. It transformed from being a highly technical and largely unapproachable wiki-style solution to becoming a pleasantly accessible solution that supports the customer experience. Like its co-founder Aaron Fulkerson, the company is a lifelong learner, steadily crafting its place and purpose in the business world and anticipating with wonder the range of possibilities yet to be discovered.

Summary: Creative Guru 101

Creativity comes from within each of us and manifests as thoughts, ideas, and actions. We are responsible and accountable for what we bring into the world. But our accelerated pace promotes a growing creative disorder where people feel disconnected and dispassionate toward the fruits of their ideation. By cultivating a beginner's mind, we can help ensure our ongoing involvement with our work.

The beginner's mind is open, teachable and free of preconceived notions. It occurs when one is in a state of mindfulness, the practice of awareness of life in the here and now. Mindfulness promotes concentration, improves comprehension, enables insight, and guards against distraction. It reboots mental processes, heightens acuity, stimulates creativity and facilitates decision making.

We live in a remarkable time in the evolution of our world with its integration of global cultures, where the mindfulness practices of Eastern traditions are readily available to us. As discerning creatives, we can fill our "toolbox" with time-tested teachings across many traditions that will help us set our intentions, align with our purpose, master our art, and craft real value in the world. To tap our artistic inspirations, we must have quiet space for reaching deeply within. This indulgence triggers discoveries, facilitates new connections, enhances learning, distills understanding, and hones craft.

Some creatives, like myself, suffer from something called the *Imposter Syndrome*. We cringe at being labeled experts when we view ourselves as earnest students constantly learning and exploring. We value maintaining a sense of humbleness around our work, but once someone identifies us as an expert, it is hard to put that label aside. We also value the freedom to try and fail, and the "expert" label seems not to allow that. There is also shame in not feeling as confident in our ability and knowledge as others might think.

Knowing and valuing the truth of our work keeps us humble and accountable. The creative process is time consuming. The ability to risk failure in a safe space in order to find ideas that work is essential. Where room for error and accountability are encouraged, thinking is more creative and strategic, confidence soars, and companies generate higher revenue. False pride can interfere with willingness to be accountable. Knowing how to fail also teaches us to know when to pull the plug on a project that isn't working.

It is important to balance our use of technology with our implementation of hands-on skills. When we are distanced from a hands-on connection with what we create, such arms-length, sensory-deprived "interaction" can result in the production of short-term junk, increased unwillingness to accept responsibility for outcomes, and decreased trust between creatives and clients. Clients like to know that the people bringing their projects to life are connected to their work at every level. Being upfront about our work builds trust because it demonstrates responsibility, shows integrity, and reveals reliability.

When businesses implement rapid prototyping at scale in order to expedite deliverables, creatives are forced to move quickly onto their next projects. The pace discourages reflection or accountability. Clients grow frustrated from lack of interest in reworking inferior ideas, and trust implodes. We must remember that the quality of our lives, of ALL life, depends on the quality and integrity of our action. It is time to awaken and be thoughtful and earnest about our work and our craft. Approach every project by engaging these two steps:

• Align with your core values—your belief system.

• Reflect on these questions:

  If quality is central to success, what must be sacrificed given the amount of time, budget and human resources?

  What will make the project successful, purposeful, and a source of pride?

  When, in the course of the project, will it be beneficial to use rapid prototyping?

7 Rules of Mastery

The Three Degrees of Motivation: High, Happy, and Passionate

At the risk of stating the obvious, we are all human. In addition, we are all individuals, which means we have evolved personal desires and aspirations based on how we view ourselves and how we want others to see us. This obsession with shaping our image to help imagine and define our world makes us homo sapiens unique. We can literally create our own reality.

We have the amazing ability to nurture and manifest our hopes and visions, transforming them into something tangible and experiential that can be shared with others on both a micro family level and on a macro global scale. As creatives, we have the skills and expertise not only to express our own visions, but to help others express their dreams as well. And in our dedication to our craft, we can achieve nothing short of mastery.

Mastery is a weighty, and perhaps even ominous word, isn't it? What sorts of feelings, emotions, sensory details and images surface when you wrestle with applying that term to your own efforts and accomplishments? Do you feel intimidated? Humbled? Confident? In awe? Do you have visions of hallowed halls and antiquity or long years of apprenticeship? Do you flash back to trial, error, dogged persistence, and long solitary hours of learning, honing, and perfecting?

The Merriam-Webster Dictionary defines *mastery* as "having knowledge and skill that allows you to do, use, or understand something very well."[61] But what the dictionary doesn't do is delve into the very heart of mastery, which is motivation itself. What drives a person to master a skill, a discipline, or an activity? What compels someone to channel their life force in such a concerted, deliberate, and refined way? How does one identify, manifest and manage their mojo in order to accomplish goals and visions. And how powerful must a motivation be to transform dedication into longevity? There is, after all, a difference, by degrees and galaxies, between prime motivators and their short- and long-term effects.

I've identified three distinct levels of motivation that I classify as follows:

Basic Procurement versus the Hot-Pursuit High:

Simply wanting something and buying it versus chasing an object of desire and attaining a high from a pursuit that actively challenges wiles and skill.

Meaning versus Happiness:

Doing something because it's meaningful versus because it affords happiness.

Passion versus Passing Fancy:

Demonstrating the perseverance born of passion and dedication versus entertaining a drive based on occasional "likes."

The Hot-Pursuit High

Some people love the chase, the thrill of going after something. It gives them the temporary high of an adrenaline rush, which occurs when the body releases the hormone epinephrine as a response to exciting situations. Increased oxygen and glucose are sent to the brain, and heart rate and blood sugar levels rise.[62] An adrenaline high can actually be addictive. How many times have we heard some people referred to as "excitement junkies."

Thrill seekers are constantly on the prowl, looking for their next high, their next opportunity to entertain risk and feel their heart pound in their chest. We have entertainment icons that model this behavior for us: James Bond, Indiana Jones, Lara Croft, Jack Sparrow, Jason Bourne, and all the other action/adventure heroes we see in movies. At some level, there's a little bit of them in each one of us. Consider Pierce Brosnan's character in *The Thomas Crown Affair* who was so bored he had to steal a painting in order to feel alive again. It was not the $10 million painting that felt rewarding to him. It was the chase that rejuvenated his mojo, tickled, and delighted him.

This same chase can be seen in entrepreneurs, VCs, real estate developers and some creative types. It's like a toxic drug that delivers a wonderful sensation, leaving a person feeling as though they can conquer the world. Then there is a drop in endorphins, a sense of going through a withdrawal, and a sudden, intense need to engage the next hunt. Some people, like Mark Zuckerberg and Sir Richard Branson, have made a career out of this need for speed, this constant pushing of limits to test possibilities, and have been seriously successful.

The opposite of the Hot-Pursuit High is the basic procurement technique of seeing something and wanting it badly enough to go out and buy it directly. There's no chase, no strategizing, no impelling force, and no competitive feeding frenzy. It's uncluttered, uncomplicated, unsexy and unremarkable. You wonder how this motivation has enough life to have legs, but it really is a matter of simply seeing, wanting, and getting, without agenda or disruptive purpose.

Meaning versus Happiness

When I first started this book project, I wondered how people can perfect skills and become the best they can be at jobs they don't even love. While doing research for this book, and meeting and interviewing people from all over the world, I learned that dedication to craft is not limited to the pursuit of one's passion. Life's highs, happiness, and deeper meaning may be realized through plying and perfecting one's craft, but meaning and purpose are not under the sole purview of craft.

Walk into any bookstore's self-help or business section and you will find a slew of books written specifically to guide people in their quest for purpose, meaning and happiness in life. I concede that I am not a guru in any of those subject areas. On the other hand, the work I do impacts people's lives in such a way that it can inform their happiness and on occasion inspire others to find their true meaning and purpose.

The search for meaning can involve contemplation and self-reflection. It is a journey that may take many years, if not an entire lifetime. Some people find meaning even in the most mundane careers. You see it every day—fathers and mothers, working two to three jobs a day, maybe 18-hour shifts, laboring nonstop until they are exhausted. They then return to their homes, feeling spent, but still need to be present for their children. I remember talking to a restaurant waiter once. He saw both my young boys and said, "Enjoy them while you can." I replied, "Yes, they grow up too fast." He said he didn't feel like he knew his children, who were now in their mid-20s. He worked three jobs throughout their infancy, toddlerhood, adolescence and teenage years to make sure they would have a college education. When they reached adulthood, they rewarded his efforts by pursuing great careers. He felt so proud. It brought me to tears. You hear this all the time. Stories of sacrifices that parents make so that their children can have better lives and greater access to opportunities.

That waiter's story represents the epitome of the American dream. He was an immigrant who came to this country believing that if he worked extremely hard, his girls could have a better future. He might identify his life purpose as being a steady provider for his family, ensuring they had shelter, education, and limitless opportunities. This role gave meaning to everything he did: Rising at 4:00 a.m. every morning; working three jobs; sacrificing his personal time and quality family time in order to ensure his family had all that they needed to live, learn and grow. I asked him if he was "happy" working those three jobs. His answer was a resounding "No."

But his love for his family and his ability to provide for them gave him satisfaction, meaning, and a sense of peace.

High levels of meaning often come at the expense of happiness. People living meaningful lives may have more stress and anxiety due to tendencies toward self-sacrifice for others. They are like Sherpas helping extreme sports enthusiasts climb Mt. Everest in order to experience a moment on top of the world. Leading psychological scientist Martin Seligman says that people who lead meaningful lives use their greatest strength and talent serving and investing in something larger than themselves, even when they know it can cost them their own happiness.

In his book *Man's Search for Meaning,* holocaust survivor Viktor Frankl, a prominent Jewish psychiatrist and neurologist, asserted that "happiness cannot be pursued; it must ensue. One must have a reason to 'be happy.'"[63] In fact, Frankl discerned that when people "pursue" happiness, it leaves them less happy. In a study published in the *Journal of Positive Psychology,* researchers found a stigma attached to the pursuit of a happy life. Happiness seekers are perceived as shallow, self-absorbed, selfish "takers" whereas people focused on leading meaningful lives are seen as "givers."[64] Meaning transcends the self, and people who cultivate meaningful lives are empathetic to those in need and find joy in doing for others.

> Meaning transcends the self and people who cultivate meaningful lives are empathetic to those in need and find joy in doing for others.

Happiness, on the other hand, is very primal and need-based. It occurs when people (or animals) get what they want and are satisfied, temporarily.[65] It is joy born of receiving benefits, which often results in an endless void that leaves them wanting more. People who eat and crave chocolate can relate to this. This motivation is not tied to helping others. Consider the "happiness" that brands and media are trying to sell us—the latest gadgets, fashions, technologies, cars, shoes, mansions, etc. Happiness is transitory. Every product has its season because the human attention span is short and the need for new prevails. Consumerism offers short-term "fixes" that cultivate perpetual appetites.

Which motivation has the greatest longevity: meaning or happiness? Well, if you ate a delicious In-N-Out burger, and its consumption made you happy, how soon before you would need another one to be happy? Almost immediately, right? On the other hand, meaning endures beyond the present moment. This longevity makes the sacrifice not only bearable, but transforms it into a contribution that bears repeating.

Passion versus Passing Fancy

Optimism and resilience are two characteristics indicative of someone possessing a passionate focus or drive. I can detect passion in a person right away. When someone confides that even after years of rejection they are still pursuing a dream because deep down it is the reason they arise each morning with complete enthusiasm, I know I have just witnessed passion. Passionate people are driven by a fire burning deep in their core. Their passion is like a double expresso, sending their hearts racing, and propelling them onward. Deep down, they know it is not enough to simply achieve their dream. They must also share it with the world. This is their oxygen. This is passion.

Unlike those moments in life when you see something you like and express a fondness for it, passion is the ingredient that enables you to navigate naysayers, stay focused through a gauntlet of impossible obstacles, keep your eye on the prize regardless of the outcome, and return to the scene of the task again and again every day until that which is so earnestly sought is hard and faithfully won. To the passionate hearted, time is irrelevant. One becomes so fully engrossed in the process it becomes self-perpetuating, deeply sustaining and boundlessly energizing.

Alternately, the occasional, non-committal "like" is not sustainable. "Like" does not inspire allegiance or any depth of feeling. "Like" is a passing fancy. Sometimes "Like" may feel like passion, and it may even inspire action and commitment for a prolonged period of time until the infatuation wears off. In such instances, it is important to recognize that the passing fancy was not a passion at all so as to stave off any sense of disappointment or failure. Those who are not fully in touch with their authentic passion may find themselves caught in the cycle of "like." Though inspired for a period of time by a passing fancy, they will quit and move on to the next promising offering or distracting twinkle on the horizon the moment they encounter any degree of resistance or need for concerted effort. This "attention deficit" pattern of behavior will lead ultimately to a hodgepodge of unfinished projects and a profound sense of having an unfinished life.

Whatever your most powerful motivation may be, finding this mojo is one of the most challenging things one can do. There are countless articles out there, preaching to the masses about quitting their jobs and finding their passion. In fact, there is an entire industry of motivational speakers and self-help gurus with their books, workshops, methodologies, and keys to better living ready to share their inspiration for crafting a meaningful life. Much of this work does have a basis in scientific research and real-world experience, and because we can now share the awareness and perspectives of global points of view derived from the philosophies, practices and traditions of many cultures, our approaches to "finding our bliss" can vary greatly. Largely, we are told that when we visualize what we want, operate from our heart space, become mindful and aware, and move toward doing that which gives us greatest joy and fulfillment, the Universe will co-create with us to make our dreams come true. People can turn their hobby into a career and manifest happiness if only they will let go of fear, have faith, and trust their gut instinct. Well, maybe.

I am very cautious about promoting this movement toward self-awareness and self-realization, where you abandon what is familiar and secure and throw yourself headlong into the abyss of possibility trusting you will be caught and cradled, nurtured and made to blossom. It's not because I don't believe in it, but because I think there can be a lot more work and possible pitfalls, and there is such a thing as personal responsibility. While I do go on stage and talk about finding your passion, and giving meaning to, and designing your life, I often have a caveat to that statement—it is not an easy road. Even *Shark Tank*'s Daymond John held down a day job at Red Lobster to make ends meet while pursuing his entrepreneurial dream.[66] Some of us may happen to envision a new way of "serving" the world that becomes really successful and lucrative, while others simply exhaust their nest eggs and have to reboot when they are close to or in their retirement age.

As a frequent keynote speaker, I find myself aligned with this unspoken oath/responsibility to share realistic insights gained from working with and designing for all sorts of people and brands. I have watched people succeed, seen people fail, and everything in between. Believe me, the grass isn't always that green on the other side. Whatever you choose to do will require effort, planning, a willingness on your part to see the world in a new way, teachability, patience, flexibility, agility, and perseverance. Following your heart is not a cakewalk, but it can lend immense depth and meaning to your life and purpose. Finding and living your passion makes you wholly responsible and accountable for crafting your life.

Mel's Motivation Matrix

Cultivating Expertise and Passion Gives Me Joy

I spend my life in a research/discovery mode. I love learning new things, perfecting new skills, and moving beyond my comfort zone so I can expand my range of possibilities. Just because you are good at something, does not mean you are necessarily passionate about it or want to make it your life's work. I know myself pretty thoroughly. I know what drives and motivates me. I am clear on what I feel passionate doing. I also am clear about the importance of cultivating new expertise to enhance my skill sets and stoke my passion for my purpose. For example, I love learning to fly, but I am not going to give up my design profession to become a commercial pilot. I may put in the time, the flight hours, the practice and repetition that helps me master any craft, but I don't have the passion necessary to want to soar into the clouds daily. Still, the experience of taking the controls and sailing up into the heavens can add new depth and perception to my sensibility as an artist/designer. If you commit yourself to something you do not absolutely love, you may one day find an excuse to depart from it. Consider a common syndrome in the Chinese adult population who, as children in a STEM academic system, were drilled endlessly to master their skill in mathematics. When they grew up, they pursued professions as doctors, physicists, and researchers. Then 30 years later, some of them experienced an awakening and discovered that their true calling was to write, paint, cook, make, or simply live another life.

In the book *Battle Hymn of the Tiger Mother,* the author Amy Chua recounts the extremes she went to in order to motivate her unwilling daughter to learn a difficult piano piece.[67] She threatened to donate her dollhouse, piece by piece, to the Salvation Army, to deny her holiday and birthday gifts, and even bathroom breaks. Eventually the child learned the piece perfectly, but the learning was not a motivation from a passionate call within. Rather, the learning was done under duress.

In my world, design is both my passion and my expertise. It gives me joy and brings meaning to my life. Because of my deep drive to create, even when there are days of complete frustration, administrative snafus, or endless meetings, I still am able to find the balance, feel the love and joy, and return to sanity. Not only does my passion for the work keep me going, but it gives me hope that I can still make a change in the decision-making process, or influence a company to go in a particular direction.

Client Interactions Provide My High

I love talking to clients, helping them figure out their next path, being part of their tribe, and consulting with them as they shape a new or improved reality.

Sparking Success in Others Makes My Life Meaningful

Seeing a client evolve from a two-person team to a $100 million company, or watching them grow individually and professionally brings satisfaction and meaning to my life and work. I thrive on the big hugs or firm handshakes I receive after a keynote engagement, when strangers approach me and reveal their most inner fears and aspirations. It heartens me to know that they have the courage to share their stories because I found the courage to share mine.

My Happiness Comes from My Children

If only we could be like little children again, with their innocence, wonder, and view of the world as wholly new and perfect. Their silly goofiness, their cries, their laughter all strike a chord in my being. They make me want to be a better mom, and a great person in general. It's their willingness to forgive, listen, discover, and their general joie de vivre, that capture my heart. When I am with them, I come alive with joy.

These Are a Few of Our Favorite Things...

{What Are Yours?}

Rules of Mastery

As you live the raw truth of your most authentic motivation, you get to practice what I call the *Rules of Mastery*, a set of guidelines for doing anything well. Employ the Rules of Mastery first on yourself as you faithfully engage your deepest drive and passion. Then, as they become second nature to you, apply them expertly to the way you choose to impact the world.

Whatever you engage in during the course of a day, from a routine task to a crafted project, every day is an opportunity to learn from successes and mistakes, and to learn new things that can inform your work. We all have good days and bad days, we enjoy when a day has been particularly productive, and we feel frustrated when we encounter hiccups and challenges. Every day affords us an opportunity to execute excellence, to move toward greater perfection, and to be of service. There is a momentum in perfecting which incites an artist (a creative thinker and doer) to wake up the next morning and do it all over again. These Rules of Mastery are a set of guidelines for anything worth doing and worth doing well. We have already touched upon them throughout our discussion in this chapter without actually calling them out.

These guidelines are personal, invite introspection and reflection, and offer the wisdom for strengthening you at your core. They are the Pilates of craftsmanship. They are not always easy, but they are always necessary. Our adherence to the rules is largely hidden as others don't see our internal drivers, our persistence, our sacrifice, our hard work and long hours, and our dedication to their needs. What they do see is what we create for them, and they reap the outcomes over time.

Rule 1: Find Your Highs/Meaning/Passion

Know yourself thoroughly. What strengthens and defeats you? What elevates and levels you? What do you love and loathe? For what do you live? How do you want to change the world? Whose life do you want to touch? Meditate deeply on what you value, what gives you joy, meaning, and purpose. Consider upfront what your expectations are, what your current responsibilities and commitments require from you, what you can live with, and what you can't live without, and then proceed to craft every moment accordingly.

Rule 2: Dedicate Your Life and Breath to Your Craft

We are in our bodies for an entire lifetime. Our process of reaping and sewing, engaging and serving, envisioning and creating is a lifelong commitment. Do you live, breathe and embody your purpose? Do you identify as one with your work? Do you have the mindset and skills to stay fresh, focused, and interested? Decide what you stand for, what it is that you want to bring forth in this life, and your plan for making that happen. This is your craft. Give yourself to it. Breathe your life force into it so that it too can live in this world.

Rule 3: Choose Your Heroes Wisely and Be That Person Who Inspires You

We all have role models in our lives who we would love to emulate. We put them on a pedestal to serve as our pillars of love and altruism, good deeds, innovation and creativity, curiosity and adventure, courage and action, and masterful accomplishment. Be selective of your heroes and icons, and let yourself be elevated by their example.

Rule 4: Be Accountable

We are the authors of our own actions. Acknowledging our works, the good and the bad, builds character, integrity, trust, and makes us more accessible and relatable. It is imperative to take ownership of our mistakes, without hesitation or thought of saving face.

Rule 5: Remember that Big Is Not Always Best

Small can be mighty. Excellence can be delivered with finesse and attention paid to the smallest of details. Nimbleness, agility, focused technique and a talent for leveraging can win the day.

Rule 6: View Each Failure as a Stepping Stone toward Constant Perfection

Sometimes we can't see what can be until we learn what doesn't work. Each failure hones and perfects our skills the way every drop of water carves the stone. There are no mistakes, only iterations toward perfection.

Rule 7: Work Hard Each Groundhog Day and Deliver the Originality Born of Quality and Consistency

If you're going to do something, give it your all. Every action is an expression of who you are. As you create, be fully in the moment with each thing that you do, even if it feels as if you do the same thing each day. Every day your work is a new and perfected signature that will touch and be recognized by someone.

Case Study: Karen Krasne, CEO of Extraordinary Desserts

The high art of pastry making is both passion and purpose to Extraordinary Desserts' owner and founder Karen Krasne. From the very start, this San Diego native has charted her own course as a self-proclaimed "global gypsy." Her passion for the exotic led her to Hawaii after high school, where she earned a Bachelor of Science degree in Food Science and Human Nutrition from the University of Hawaii before moving to Paris to study baking at Le Cordon Bleu. Karen frequently returns to France to train with masters at Lenotre and Bellouet Conseil. Travel and immersion have brought awareness and inspiration, and helped Karen identify and express, in delicious ways, her own artistic vision and craft.

At Extraordinary Desserts, Karen creates pastry perfections that delight the senses, excite the imagination, and feed the soul. The art of fine desserts is by nature impermanent, but the joy they can bring to special occasions lasts well beyond the last crumb on the plate. The motto at Extraordinary Desserts is "Indulge, Celebrate, and Love the Moment." Karen and her gifted team all strive daily to embody and perpetuate that maxim for themselves personally. She believes that if they live that way, then they also bring that spirit into the restaurants and share its essence with others.

Karen believes that the foundation and starting point of her success is having a healthy body and mind. She begins each day with meditation, yoga and exercise. Taking that special time out for her own self-care leaves her poised and available for all that can happen during a day and night of work. Observing this daily routine helps her achieve balance in all of her roles: as a CEO, a mom, a creative, a wife, and a student of life.

Money has never been the motivation behind Karen's work. Her passion for pastry making is organic. For a long time, Karen avoided committing her creative effort to a brick-and-mortar structure. She did not want to be tied down or to have her inspiration suppressed in any way. She did not like making cookies, pies, or donuts. She specialized in cakes: elaborate, fanciful cakes with finely crafted layers of ineffable deliciousness all topped with a seductive fusion of Hawaiian and Parisian exquisiteness. But the demand for her sweet delicacies grew beyond the capacity of her Dad's kitchen and garage, so she relented and opened her first pastry shop in the San Diego community of Hillcrest.

Today, this lover of ponchos and pastries, Weimaraner dogs and Wade Hoefer landscape paintings has a team of 120 employees in several locations including San Diego's Little Italy and Hillcrest. She ensures continuity in the quality of her artfully crafted product, her vision, and her brand voice by hiring artisans who desire to learn and grow, and who possess an underlying passion for desserts. Karen's kitchen is female-based. Most are mothers, and together they have created a support system that is like a family. Together, everyone operates according to four embedded core values:

1. Passion: They bring enthusiasm and drive to all they do.

2. Openness: They appreciate other perspectives and different opinions.

3. Understanding: They are committed to learning all that they can about their business.

4. Respect: Team members never take one another or their guests for granted.

As a CEO and kitchen boss, Karen is tough but fair. She expects loyalty, a strong work ethic and solid team skills. Karen jumps right in and works alongside her staff, so that together they imbue their creations with personality, complexity, and amazing flavor and fancifulness.

The experience of "delight," according to Karen, is essential not only to her craft, but also to feeding and entertaining people in general. As a hands-on owner and craftsperson, Karen is always seeking ways to take her creations to the next level. Inspiration can find its spark almost anywhere if one is open to the awareness. It can be found in the discovery of a new wine, in the sweetness of a song, walking the dogs, or watching a child grow up. Our world is a celebration of sensory magnificence, and it all can be translated, through the finely tuned artistic vision of a pastry craftsperson, into a rich and refined delicacy. Karen continually raises the bar for herself and her staff, finding captivating ways to blow her customers' minds, make them speechless, and assure them they are experiencing something extraordinary.

Summary: Rules of Mastery

The human species is uniquely gifted in that we can literally create our own reality. Creatives can express their visions and help others express their dreams. As dedicated craftspeople, we achieve mastery. *The Merriam-Webster Dictionary* defines *mastery* as "having knowledge and skill to do, use, or understand something very well." But the heart of mastery is motivation, of which I've identified three distinct levels:

• Basic Procurement versus Hot Pursuit High

• Meaning versus Happiness

• Passion versus Passing Fancy

The hot pursuit high is motivation for thrill seekers like VCs, real estate developers and some entrepreneurs looking for risk and some extreme level of engagement in order to feel alive. The opposite of this motivation is basic procurement, which is as simple and unsexy as seeing something, wanting it, and going out and buying it.

People motivated by meaning use their strength and talent to serve and invest in something larger than themselves, even at the expense of their own happiness. Meaning endures beyond the present moment, so the sacrifice is made more bearable. People motivated by happiness are answering a primal need, and the satisfaction is temporary.

Passion is an all-consuming fire burning deep in a person's core. It is their reason for waking up, their oxygen, and their impetus for action. Passion enables a person to focus, defy obstacles, and be totally engaged in a flow where time is irrelevant.

Those motivated by passing fancy find themselves caught up in a cycle of "like," without any real sense of allegiance or loyalty and an innate willingness to totter after the next distracting twinkle on the horizon.

It is important to know your level of motivation, and there are lots of programs and books to show you how to craft a meaningful life by living your passion. I can tell you that finding your passion, giving meaning to it, and designing your life is not an easy road. Whatever you choose to do will require effort, planning, and perseverance. Following your heart can lend immense depth and meaning to your life and purpose. Finding and living your passion makes you wholly responsible and accountable for crafting your life.

There is a difference between expertise and passion. Doing something well may not be fulfilling. Doing something meaningful rewards one's sense of purpose. Live the raw truth of your most authentic motivation. Use the following Rules of Mastery as guidelines for doing something meaningful and doing it well:

1. Find your highs/meaning/passion.

2. Dedicate your life and breath to your craft.

3. Choose your heroes wisely and be that person that inspires you.

4. Be accountable.

5. Remember that big is not always best.

6. View each failure as a stepping stone to perfection.

7. Work hard and deliver originality, quality, and consistency.

8 *Craft Value*

Know Your Power

When Moira Forbes invited me to attend the Forbes Women's Summit in 2015, for my second year in a row, I found myself among women leaders in the fields of finance, politics, business, arts, medicine, and technology. The Summit sizzled with the energy of accomplishment and dynamic purpose, and I found myself surrounded by noteworthy, high-powered CEOs including Sara Blakely, Jessica Alba, Chelsea Handler, and Ivanka Trump, to name a few.

When all the buzz and adrenaline settled, I began to wonder why exactly Moira Forbes had invited me to this elite gathering? I am not Paula Scher or Zaha Hadid. I am just a Malaysian-born Chinese immigrant who happens to be a designer. All of a sudden, I felt a strange sensation in my stomach. The imposter syndrome crept in and engulfed me. This widespread psychological phenomenon is characterized by an inability to internalize accomplishments, which I touched on earlier in the book, resulting in a lack of confidence in one's achievements, and feelings of inadequacy, fraudulence, and not belonging. This syndrome is arson to accomplishment. It sweeps like wildfire through the psyches of smart, successful, professional women. I decided that if Tina Fey, Sheryl Sandberg, Michelle Pfeiffer, Kate Winslet, Meryl Streep, and Dr. Margaret Chan, Chief of the World Health Organization can all experience the confidence thief that causes them to question their talent, validity and impact, Mel Lim at least keeps the best of company.

I did not have long to ponder the waves of phoniness and self-doubt washing through me. All that interior interloper talk disappeared as soon as Nancy Pelosi gave a powerful short speech about power. The takeaway line from it all for me was, "Know your power...and be ready."

Wow. At that moment, awareness dawned like an anvil of understanding. I knew that the 200 of us who had the good fortune to be present at that conference were there for a reason. We had something to learn from each other, to teach others, and to share. We were there because our personal experiences, with all our advances and adversities, had propelled us to achieve remarkable things in life and now the time had come for us to pay-it-forward in some fashion or another.

We've Got the Power...

Let's explore the expansive potential of our "is-ness." We are going to examine our inherent power as creatives: our ability to influence, change, and even control our environment and our world through our persuasiveness and charisma, our skills and expertise, and the degree to which we choose to confer rewards.

Over the course of my 20 years here in the United States, I have designed experiences that invite and inspire people to shop, gamble, play, walk more, walk less, talk louder, talk softly, eat more, eat less, eat fast, smile more, be serious, be happy, be focused, click here, click there, download this, right-click here, go there, do this, listen up, act now, spend more, and save, save, save. What's more, I have exercised this power at an almost incomprehensibly large and connected global scale.

The sensory nature of a creative person's work makes it inherently attractive as people yearn for innovative and imaginative products and experiences that have heart and authenticity. People have their antennas out, searching environments for that which rings true for them. We unleash our messages for their consideration, consumption and subsequent action. As a designer, I have the ability to persuade, to instigate change, to create new realities, to make and break businesses, to influence and to lead. I have real POWER. I temper my awareness of that with humility. It is incumbent upon me and upon all "influencers" to wield our power wisely, ethically, thoughtfully, and compassionately. Historic figures such as Lord Melbourne, Winston Churchill, Teddy Roosevelt, Franklin D. Roosevelt, and even Uncle Ben in Spiderman have all suggested that "the possession of great power necessarily implies great responsibility."

Transform Power into Empowerment

I cannot emphasize enough the importance of recognizing and understanding the very real power we possess and our potential as change agents. We truly touch and impact people's lives. Political and corporate strategists and behaviorists might view that sort of power as a valuable tool for directing outcomes and achieving goals, but when gain is the motivation for exercising power, people and their stories get lost. The focus becomes less on the individual and more on the masses, on revenue streams, and on guiding social and market trends. So, again, what do we do with the awareness of our power? How do we mindfully wield innovation and influence? Do we charge in, implement our creative concepts, and wait for the outcome, hoping that the emphasis will be more on our success as opposed to the value and meaning we bring the people we serve? Do we flex our creative muscles because we can, because it will profit us ultimately, or because it is the right thing to do?

Return immediately to your artisan roots and the sensory nature of all art and creativity. As people born to interpret and create, our first task and priority is to listen.

The power smoldering in our creative fingertips is not about us. It is about the clients and communities we serve. If we are listening carefully and paying attention, our applied talents and abilities gain strength and momentum through our relationship, interaction, and collaboration with those we serve.

Yes, we must listen. It is more than just wisdom, good manners, strategic engagement or smart business. It is an act of radical empowerment that promotes responsibility, reliability, productivity, efficiency, decision making, profitability, positive relationships and community. Active listening is an essential component in communication. For the creative, there are two sides to listening, both of which culminate in a greater sense of "knowing."

First, we listen to ourselves. We connect with our own needs, values, expectations, rules of mastery and engagement, mission, goals and objectives, short- and long-term vision, and core skills, abilities, and expertise. This internal assessment enables us to approach any situation with a clear idea of who we are, how we work, the magnitude of our power, and what we have to offer. It nurtures awareness in us that every moment brings growth, new learning, and infinite opportunity and potential.

Then, we listen to our clients. By showing genuine interest and listening deeply, we take those first steps in earning and instilling trust. Listening demonstrates that we are open to feedback and criticism. And perhaps most of all, listening reveals that we put the client first. Our work is not about us; it is about them. So, we take time to truly understand their needs, wants, and hopes. We learn their history, their vision, their values and what they hold dear, how they view themselves, and how they would like to be perceived. All of these information elements must be coded into the nucleus of our seed of creation as we begin to design solutions that have merit, impact, and real value.

The Story of Value and the Value of Stories

Value is a judgment of what is important, beneficial, of merit or worth, or useful. Our values inform what we create, and our designs and innovations can influence values and value. When we infuse what we value into a creative solution, we create a brand, product, or service with both an inherent and potential value. What's more is that we give something a history, a process, and a story worth telling.

Up until recently, the value of my profession—design—wasn't taken seriously enough to warrant corporations hiring Chief Creative Officers, or to even give design firms a seat at the table. But something has changed. Over the last 15 years, businesses have progressed. They now have irrefutable awareness of the value of great design:

McKinsey | Lunar Design
Delloite | Doblin, Digicon, Ubermind, Banyan Branch, Aqua Media
Accenture | Fjord
Capital One | Adaptive Path
Square | 80/20
Google | Mike & Maaike, Gecko Design
Facebook | Teehan + Lax, Hot Studio

It is no longer a question of whether or not design is valued. Any company or brand that is focused on growth, scaling, innovation, and brand longevity will eventually invest in design. It is just a matter of when the investment will happen. For this reason, designers must have an understanding of what businesses and their customers value and find meaningful.

Creatives as a whole need to plumb the depths of their customer base to understand intrinsic drivers, the core and lifeblood of which are values. Values may be of an aesthetic nature. They may have an ethical or social activist base. They may be bottom-line or goal driven. They may have a company or community focus. They may be experiential, imbuing a sense of meaning and purpose. Demonstrating to customers that you have listened and you know them builds trust and loyalty. Delivering creative solutions that reflect a customer's values suggests that you have touched their pulse; they have been seen, heard, and understood. When you emulate, you ingratiate. The other thing that happens as you craft according to values to create value in a product, service, or experience is that you imbue it with a story. And everyone responds to a story that resonates.

We pursue our craft in a global marketplace of people from many cultures. Every culture is celebrated, maintained and even governed by the stories of its creation, triumphs and tragedies. We all herald from cultures that have observed rich traditions of passing down stories and myths that teach us about ourselves, where we came from, who we are, and what we value. Stories are imbued with patterns. When we learn the patterns, we recognize the stories, and we understand the culture and what is expected. The patterns become guideposts for our lives and everything we do, from our daily routines to our grand adventures and our search for purpose and meaning. So, if we really wish to know and understand our clients and their needs and expectations, we listen, and we learn their stories.

The Time/Value Tango

For the past four years, I've been researching brands and interviewing customers. In my research, I discovered a common denominator in value creation: TIME. This is the new value currency in an accelerated world. Time is money, which then translates into advantage, opportunity, clout, efficiency and facility for businesses, customers, designers and creatives. Translated, it is simple economics: the more time that gets built into a project, the more money the project costs. Let me break it down:

WHAT BUSINESSES WANT

Businesses in general care about people, products, cash and customers, goals and objectives:

- Sales

- Profits

- Growth

- Scale

- Global Domination

- Brand Longevity

WHAT CUSTOMERS WANT

Customers care about the How, Why, and What of deliverables:

- Service

- Quality

- Pricing

- Cause & Stance

- Customer Experience

- Delivery

Now let's see how Time fits into the equation for everyone:

BUSINESSES WANT

- To build products and services…quickly

- To convert customers…quickly

- To grow…quickly

- To win…quickly

- To profit…quickly

CUSTOMERS WANT

- Family/personal time—now

- Tools to make job performance faster, easier, and more efficient—now

- More time in a day to do what is most desired—now

- The things they buy to work and LAST—ASAP

- Enriching experiences—now and perpetually

Time-related questions that designers, innovators, and other creatives hear often:

- "Can you make users download faster?"

- "Can you make users click the Buy Now button faster?"

- "Can you help customers make their purchasing decision faster?"

- "Can you help customers prolong their experience?"

- "Can you make users stay longer on our website?"

Value then, in our time-starved world, comes from our ability as creatives to manipulate time. We have the power to shape how people spend their time. And yet we also want our work to expand into a realm of greater significance and dimensionality than simply speed and efficiency. Value is personal, and craftsmanship (which builds additional value by deepening the meaning of a brand, product or service through the investment of time and hands-on processes) imparts uniqueness, thoughtful creation, and honed holism. Building value through the application of craftsmanship reveals a commitment to high standards and a realization that fast and first are not always future-focused or lasting.

If you consider craft to be an essential part of your core offering to clients and to your reputation as an artisan of exceptional innovations and designs, do your very best to educate your clients about how craft lends an indelible uniqueness, authenticity, and aesthetic value to every project. In fact, it causes us to reflect upon our own lives as craft. Some will have neither the patience nor the budget for such meticulous executions, but others will have a deep respect for the application of care and precise detail given to their product or design solution. Crafting value suggests to others that you have an appreciation for the art of living, that you don't settle for anything less than the best your clients deserve, and that you have a deep understanding that what you express to the world influences everything in a transformative way. Crafting value is about so much more than concerns about time and money or strategizing processes for the assemblage of pre-designed parts. It reveals an understanding of the nature of existence in the deepest way, an awareness of purpose, the ability to distinguish the necessary from the incidental, and a reverence for essence.

Crafting Experiences

The latest buzzword in the quest for happiness/meaning is "experience." The newest research out indicates that now people care to pursue life enriching and enhancing experiences, and they know there is no time like the present. They want to climb Everest, take a tour of outer space, hike the Appalachian Trail all the way through from Georgia to Maine, go on a themed cruise to an exotic location, raft down rivers in Thailand, take an African safari, vacation in a treehouse, etc.

People have a heightened awareness of the value and brevity of life. They have identified the revocable time contract with which they were born into this life, and they have a pronounced realization that the meter on their activity clock can expire at any time. Hence, we have a new wave of agencies and designers with titles like Chief Experience Officer.

I am an accomplice here, helping people and families prolong their experiences, whether it is purchasing something or downloading something, or simply crafting memories. In the journal *Psychological Science,* researchers Matthew Killingsworth, Thomas Gilovich, and Amit Kumar assert that spending money on experiences provided more enduring happiness than acquiring impulse purchases.[68] Experiences can be planned for and anticipated over time. This gives them longer life, builds excitement, allows for conjecture about outcomes, inspires conversations, and puts people in a happier and more generous frame of mind.

This may also be part of the attraction of crafting a meaningful life and exploring entrepreneurial ventures. There is an experiential quality to crafting a life that has meaning and purpose. What you get is always much more than you could ever have anticipated, and the stories that emerge, for better or worse, are always interesting to tell.

Where happiness is derived from purchasing material goods, there is no mystery. What you see is what you get. Which is why, as designers and creatives, it is incumbent upon us to craft value into products and services so that they have a history, a process, a story worth telling. I see material goods as having intrinsic value when they are well crafted. Their longevity in lives and households makes it possible for memories to grow up around them. Some even enjoy heirloom legacies and stories. My mom's Chanel purse (the subject of this chapter's case study) is a classic example. It has proven to be a timeless piece that has provided pride in ownership, withstood the test of time, conjured fond memories of my mother, is still backed by its brand, and carries added monetary and historic value.

Crafting Brands that Stick

Branding is beyond surface cosmetic value. We all know that. But it is harder than ever now to challenge the status quo, to come up with differentiators, when everyone else is humming the same tune. Add to that the noise factor of social media, digital media, new startups, new ideas, and newer, more enticing, cheaper competition. Every day, clients ask me a barrage of questions:

How do we stand apart? How do we make sure our brand has value? How do we manage social media to generate brand awareness, customers, and revenue? How do we make sure that our brand (not necessarily the product itself) stays relevant for the next 10 years?

Those questions are relevant in this age where being "relevant" and "meaningful" come in various forms of "importance." Long gone are the days where a good brand was automatically the result of a good product offering. I would like to think that connection still exists, but the reality is that with money and social media clout/influence, one can look past the core of the business, and the efficiency of the product, especially if the product is being endorsed by celebrities. It is as though we have accepted mediocrity as the new standard. A good example of this is our growing appetite for junk news. We are so blinded by reality TV and the barrage of headlines the media endlessly blasts at us, that our discernment filters are overrun. We forget or are too overwhelmed to question the authenticity of the sources, the news. We take it all in and accept what we are fed.

Part of our job as creatives and design leaders is to also be educators. Despite the numbing anesthetic of reality television, people are clamoring for consciousness and yearning to be awakened and fulfilled in ways they had never dreamed. People want to be a part of something real and bigger than themselves. Deep down they want to know that the things they do every day are going to have a positive impact all around. With an environment that is stressed, and with global cultures suddenly lashed together and having to figure out how to mesh and get along, a greater mindfulness is needed all the way around. People must consider deeply the impact of the words they say, the modes of transportation they use, the greenness of the homes in which they live, the sustainability of the products they purchase and the energy they use, their level of consumption of finite resources, and the list goes on.

In crafting brands for our world today, we must move beyond profit motive as our reason and call to action and address the issue of mass consumption and the unchecked draining of precious resources. As we have all heard it said, necessity is the mother of invention and scarcity promotes innovation. It is important to position rule-breaking brands that challenge the "bigger is better" mindset in a way that rewards mindful choices as opposed to appealing to consumer guilt or shame. Crafting brands for today is intrinsic to our greater calling of carefully crafting a world that will not just survive, but will also thrive. Brands that are gutsy, agile and ingenious and embrace global views, maximize resources, preserve the endangered, and tenaciously adopt frugal innovation (which focuses on affordability, quality, simplicity and sustainability) can ultimately transform our throwaway society. Consumers can move away from their super-sized, I-want-it-now mindset into a more expansive earth- and social-wise paradigm that values longevity and retention and demands lifestyle enhancers that embody the beneficial. In raising our standards and designing with an awareness of the "whole," we can drive brand, product, and social value, and give a new and more pristine meaningfulness to the term "service offering."

The breakneck competition that percolates around us, even though we have confidence in our vision, values, direction, and capabilities, can leave us feeling like strangers in a strange land. For all the connectivity in the world, we can feel startling disconnected. What can give new life and purpose in our work is the awareness that we are artisans of a new and more mindful reality. Our actions, and everything that we innovate and craft into being, have a very decided impact on the future of design, business, consumerism, the social fabric, and the life and health of the planet. We can no longer have the luxury of thinking in the micro. We must take everything to the macro level, because that is the base of the proverbial hill where everything rolling downhill lands.

Case Study: The Lim Family's Chanel Bag

I have made dedication to craft integral to my professional work and continuing growth and development as an industry leader. As someone committed to having a lasting impact in the world through my mindful endeavors, I understand that thoughtful creation and attention to detail transform energy output into artisan effort. I practice rules of mastery. I am passionate about and dedicated to my craft. I focus on the details and take ownership. I understand that big is not always best, and I view successes and failures all as stepping stones toward perfection. My commitment to craftsmanship is ingrained at a foundational level. My training began early in life with my mother who served as my teacher and role model.

I would describe my mother as a fashionista. She grew up amongst nine siblings and was the eldest in a very traditional family. After completing high school, she worked in sales in order to help support the family, and never had the opportunity to attend college. I remember that whenever my sister or I didn't eat our dinner, my mother would remind us of how she had started working at the age of nine to support all of her siblings. She labored endlessly so that my aunts and uncles didn't have to, and she helped put them through school. One ended up in an Ivy League school, and one became a high court judge.

My mom worked hard her entire life. She built a company from scratch that blossomed into one of the most well-known furniture manufacturers in Asia. After 20 years of cultivating her career, she reached the point where she was doing really well. She was traveling around the world, and finally started treating herself to some of the better things in life. She had a sharp eye for fashion finery of exceptional value. Chanel, Escada, Dior, Saint Laurent and Versace all graced her closet.

When my mother passed away in 2010, she left her "vintage" couture accessories and clothing to me and my sister Wendy. One of these treasured items was a Chanel maxi/jumbo flap bag circa 1990. I didn't give much thought to "the bag" until I hit a point in my career where, similar to my mother, I began treating myself occasionally to beautiful designer fashions. I thought I would buy some Chanel, and remembering my Mom's old bag, I decided to take it with me to the Chanel store at South Coast Plaza in Orange County, California.

The bag was old and loved enough that the authentication number had already worn off. Regardless, the

Chanel specialist examined the piece and decided to accept it for restoration/refurbishment. They made no guarantee, but they agreed to replace the strap, redip the gold buckles, and possibly redye the lamb skin.

While waiting for the outcome of what would be a 12-week restoration process, I began to wonder what other brands out there would take back a product after 25 years, without proof of purchase or legible authentication number, and work to restore it as a piece of art and quality craftsmanship. And who of sane mind would assume the potential liability of ruining a vintage heirloom? It caused me to reflect on my own company's brand and whether, as a service provider, I stood by my work in the remarkable way that Chanel does. It confirmed for me that craft and value begin within. Great brands evolve conscientiously, with an adherence to principles, highest standards, and commitment to excellence, from product/service ideation, to manufacturing, to delivery to and engagement with the end user. The entire experience inspired me, and renewed my commitment to brand excellence.

On Mother's Day of 2015, the manager at Chanel notified me that my restored bag was ready for pickup. It was a memorable occasion for me, and all the while I thought about my mom, her legacy, what she had passed down to her daughters, and how I hoped to bequeath the exquisite accessory to someone in my own family someday. I was astonished at the great care and attention shown to my vintage piece. It was as if Chanel was as sentimental about its own craftsmanship as I was sentimental about the memories and history that my mother's bag held for me. The bag looked brand new and radiated Chanel perfection.

Jumpstarting Your Value Vision

If you're wondering where to begin, I have a few thoughts that might help you jumpstart your realignment toward innovating and creating for greater meaning and value:

1. Slow down, listen, and reassess your vision and values.

2. Live deeply knowing that life is our toolbox and we must fill it with sensory experiences.

3. Lend empathy, relevance and connection to everything you do.

4. Break rules, take risks, and challenge the status quo to craft a more authentic existence.

5. DON'T DRINK THE KOOLAID!!!

6. Craft value and value craft.

7. Embody the creative process and the highest standards possible, and be the champion of global-centered design.

8. Impart uniqueness and thoughtful creation into your work, and innovate wisely to lessen your footprint while solidifying your imprint.

9. Build in quality and stand fully behind your creations so they endure the test of time.

10. Be the conduit between money and value.

11. Know that something of value may cost more to create initially, but something of no value may cost considerable sums in the long run.

Summary: Craft Value

Creatives all have something to learn from one another, to teach one another and to share. With our skills and expertise, we have the power to persuade, influence, change, create new realities, control our environment, make or break businesses, and lead. We are change agents with real power. As influencers, we must wield our power wisely, ethically, thoughtfully and compassionately, as every action has a global impact in today's world.

As consummate craftspeople, our first job is to listen. It is essential to communication and an act of radical empowerment. We must first listen to ourselves and conduct our own internal needs/goals assessment. Then we must listen deeply to our clients because our work is ultimately about and for them.

Listening implies that we are taking in someone's story, history and values, all of which inform our creative solutions. Listening builds trust. Clients understand they have been heard when your creative solutions reflect their values back to them.

One common denominator in value creation is "Time." As creatives in a time-starved world, we manipulate time and also have the power to shape how people spend their time. Craftsmanship is an investment of time and hands-on processes. We build value through our commitment to high standards and the premise that fast and first are not always future-focused or lasting. Craft lends an indelible uniqueness, authenticity, and aesthetic value to every project. It suggests an appreciation for the art of living, and reveals an awareness of purpose and reverence for essence.

Time also factors into the crafting of experiences. People have a heightened awareness of the value and brevity of life and are keenly pursuing life-enriching and enhancing experiences that will provide more enduring happiness than impulse purchases. Experiences can be planned for and anticipated over time, which gives them longer life, builds excitement, inspires conversations, and creates stories.

Crafting brands that have value today goes well beyond presenting a good and timely product. Part of our job as creatives is to also be educators. We are artisans of a new and more mindful reality. We can no longer think in the micro. All that we innovate and craft into being has a very decided impact on the future of design, business, consumerism, the social fabric, and the life and health of the planet. Creatives and clients alike are answering a deeper calling and engaging brands that embrace global views, maximize resources, preserve the endangered, and tenaciously adopt frugal innovation.

Knowing that everyone wants to be part of something meaningful and bigger than themselves, it is important to craft brands that enable people to align with and embody this deep-seated need. Know that value costs, but no value costs more. Great brand experiences win brand loyalty and multiply the customer base. I have shared my story with at least 20 other friends, and at least half of them have become fans of Chanel. This is a brand that understands its people, culture, history and traditions. It is a brand that has stood the test of time, and has been able to create meaning through the longevity of its product designs and history. It is a brand that has provided an aspirational, real-world example to me about the importance of craftsmanship, delivering on a brand promise, and cultivating customer loyalty and engagement. When you begin by crafting value, you ensure art for life.

9   *Be the Turtle*

Finding Longevity in the World of Impermanence

Brands come and go. Companies come and go. People come and go. We live and we die. We are all part of the cycle of life that promises us only one thing: a shelf life. In a world of constant change, impermanence is the only constant. The wisest way is to live gracefully in the NOW, extracting the sweetness of every moment. We have the power to choose. If we choose to be present, to be here NOW, we benefit by absorbing the joy in life, allowing it to enrich and nourish us in our time of being.

And yet, across cultures and regions and throughout their history and folklore, we learn of quests for the elixir of immortality: Spanish explorer Juan Ponce de Leon sought the Fountain of Youth; Adam and Eve ate of the fruit of the Tree of Life; Greek gods consumed nectar and ambrosia; Zoroastrian and Vedic mythologies refer to drinking Soma and Haoma for immortality; Hindu gods drank the nectar Amrita; the Chinese consumed "Peaches of Immortality"; in medieval times, alchemists prized the Elixir of Life created by dropping the Philosopher's Stone into mercurial water; and more recently, Indiana

Jones embarked on the quest for the Holy Grail.[69] This notion of living forever in bodies that are both beautiful and healthy has been around for thousands of years. We yearn to live and stay perpetually young, vibrant, energetic, and powerful. One only has to look at the booming fitness and cosmetic surgery industries to gauge our obsession with eternal youth. I understand and can relate. I pay $100 monthly for a small bottle of anti-aging cream and generously lather on that liquid gold, no matter the cost. Only time will tell if it's working. Of course we want to personally stick around and see how all the stories of life around us unfold, and we want to have quality of life and arresting good looks the entire time we are here on this plane of existence. That's just our narcissism around our private personas. When it comes to our professional lives, we have our smooth skin in that game as well.

Our focus as creatives is not so much about yearning for product or brand immortality. Rather, we care to ensure product, service, or brand longevity and consistently deliver on a brand promise, without compromising quality. We struggle with the trend toward inferior quality and premature brand obsolescence. All that wastefulness is conditioned by the fast-track fury around us where brands, products and services exist briefly and either break in two days or succumb to consumer addiction for the next best thing. How do you design a brand, product, or service today for longevity or emotional attachment when almost everything gets discarded in two years? Some products will come and go in the space of time it takes to answer this question.

Longevity versus Obsolescence

Most of us suspect that major companies and industries operate according to a strategy where obsolescence is built into their product cycle. We see it and pay for it, all the time. The moment you step into a store and buy a laptop computer, a newer version comes out within six months or less. Then you berate yourself for not waiting a little longer before making your purchase. It's really not your fault and there is never a perfect time to exercise your consumer muscle.

Buying a new car offers a similar experience. You walk in, pay $50K, and leave with a car that is now worth $40K, once you drive it off the lot. Then, just as the warranty matures, the car breaks down. Own it a while, and you discover you can no longer get parts for it. Depending on the product's longevity and/or the brand's strength, you can expect either a high resale value OR a lousy one. Ultimately you feel like the value of your money has diminished somehow.

While brands yearn for a long-lasting presence, and to own the market share, expected product obsolescence is another method of building anticipation for the next iteration of WOW, while allowing the current product to have a "natural" death. The iPhone series is a case in point. After a few months with their newer, better, more features than before mobile phone, customers begin to get excited after hearing the market buzz that there's a new and improved and even more remarkable version on the horizon.[70] Of course everyone wants and needs to keep up with technology. Otherwise, however will they be assured of synching seamlessly with all their other devices? The loyal customer feels the need to replace, replenish, and stay on top, in the know, and absolutely current. It illustrates our throwaway society's branding brainwash. We have cultivated a craving, an addiction to an entirely unsustainable product innovation and delivery chain. We are promised the latest and greatest, all that is newer, better, faster, sleeker, and more advanced, at the cost of quality, longevity, and vital natural resources.[71]

This approach to brand building is actually the antithesis of the old-fashioned (craftsman) way of building brand longevity. In the craftsman tradition, products lasted a long time, and came with lifetime warranties and lifetime support (and even beyond). Sometimes those warranties and support were honored for generations. Chanel's beautifully executed restoration of my deceased mother's vintage handbag offers a superb example of how a brand stands behind its products decades after an initial purchase. But over the years, like everything else, companies have discontinued "lifetime coverage," as products die "naturally" far too quickly. Then you are left having to weigh whether or not to buy a new one or repair the old.

I witnessed my own mother's furniture design company go through this crisis. My mother's company made furniture that lasted an exceptionally long time. Even if a product endured great wear and tear, my mother would take the furniture back (say it was a sofa), recondition the leather, restitch wherever necessary, and sometimes replace the sofa completely, because she stood behind her product. Then over the years, she started seeing her competition selling cheaply made Italian leather sofas for half the price, and customers were willing to pay for inferior quality, fully knowing that there was no comparison between her furniture and the lesser product. My mom began to doubt herself and questioned her commitment to craftsmanship and the products she created. She wondered if her leather sofas should have a life expectancy. She struggled with whether or not she should design them with flaws, so they would fail prematurely and customers would come in and buy replacements. It was hard to see this woman of great integrity and dedication to craft and service wrestle with her own value system as a result of market pressure.

Keeping Up with the Jones's Junk

The market trend of mediocre is an unsustainable strategy with a schlock value that bulges landfills. The United States alone, in its love affair with disposable rather than durable, produces 500 million+ tons of trash annually, which is a third of all the waste generated around the world. While we comprise just 5% of the people on the earth, we are world trash champions with mountains of toxic waste and an environment depleted of natural resources.[72] Each one of us has a personal lifetime contribution of 102 tons of garbage.[73] Put that in your doggy bag for digesting later.

Given the amount of waste we generate, brands and consumers must place product sustainability at its manufacturing and consumption core. Brands must connect to people's value systems and not just appeal to their guilt. And since for many consumers saving money is their number one concern, businesses must rethink their approach to revenue generation and methods of product manufacturing. They must begin incorporating green production techniques in their processes, which can be done on a large scale for cost efficiencies. If we make durable products that we repair when broken, brands then can make their profits through offering follow-up services. Essentially we create a service economy where both brands and consumers win.[74]

Considering the state of the environment—the sobering reality of climate change, the poisoning of the oceans, our living within the largest mass extinction ever, and the ongoing destruction of our rainforests (but don't let that worry you), it may very well be in our global best interests to create green, sustainable products that last. Perhaps it is time to look up from our all-absorbing screens and realize that our very survival on this planet requires a movement of mindfulness, where we truly recognize how our individual (consumption) behaviors impact all that is on a collective basis. Consider whether it might be time to incorporate, on a systemic level, a durable goods society that expands quality of life beyond just a financial focus. With a projected world population of over 8 billion people by 2020, we cannot continue to mass produce and throw away all in the same breath.[75] Such monumental wastefulness must cease as it is unsupportable on any level, be it social, economic, or environmental. It is time to face and curb our human addiction to all things new, learn moderation, and adopt sustainable behaviors.

Tales from the Finite: Making Sustainable Attainable

Irishman Mark Boyle, a former manager of a large organic food company, took his thoughts about sustainability a little further. Following a discussion with friends over wine aboard his yacht, Boyle wondered about the root cause of all the world's major issues. He concluded that money was the culprit and that our system of consumerism and environmental destruction requires infinite growth on a planet with finite resources. It is simply not sustainable. Boyle, who holds a business and economics degree, decided to experiment. He chose to live for a period of time without an income or any money to spend.[76]

Noting that 90% of our species' time on this planet was spent living without money, Boyle was curious to see how greatly money separates us from our ability to forage, perceive real value, survive, and thrive. According to Boyle, "The degrees of separation between the consumer and the consumed have increased so much that it now means we're completely unaware of the levels of destruction and suffering embodied in the 'stuff' we buy." We are out of touch with nature, with one another, and with real happiness and appreciation for life. Boyle suggests that if we grew our own food, we wouldn't throw a third of it away. If we made our own furniture, we would be less inclined to dispose of it every time we wanted to "redecorate." And if we had to clean our own drinking water, we would be much more mindful about ever polluting it in the first place with chemicals, feces, garbage, etc. After a year of living mindfully and "off the grid," he found he was happier, had more friends, and was in the best physical shape of his life. Slowing down, stepping out of the world of money and business, growing his own food, living in a caravan, riding a bike, and being a "maker" of his own life deprived him only of stress, utility bills, rush hour traffic snarls, and an occasional brew at the pub.[77]

Granted, the vast majority of us are not going to change our lives in the extreme way Boyle explored for himself. But there are ways in which we as individuals, as companies, as residents of a global community and planetary home can live, work, play and craft our lives and work more mindfully and sustainably.

For 30 years, Eileen Fisher, Chief Creative Officer of EILEEN FISHER, INC, a clothing company renowned for simple yet elegant designs, has worked to fashion a company committed to collaboration, community and connection. Starting in 1984, with $350 in the bank, Fisher built a company that grosses $350 million in sales, stands as a leader in human rights and social responsibility, and actively works to minimize environmental impact. The company sources organic and sustainable fibers for its clothing made in the United States. Its GREEN EILEEN recycling program takes back and resells its clothing in support of causes benefiting women and girls. The company's policies, values and initiatives all evolve from deep thinking and communicating company wide. Through this honest, empowering, transparent and co-creative business paradigm, the non-profit EILEEN FISHER Community Foundation and the EILEEN FISHER Leadership Institute, a girls' summer program, have also emerged. At EILEEN FISHER, where there is total awareness that the future depends on the choices we make today, sustainability is an inside-out and an outside-in job.[78]

Having an awareness that impermanence is the law and change is a constant, we can enhance the quality of our lives, our ability to touch and be touched, and the art of listening and understanding if we just slow down. Taking time to do things as opposed to blasting through them while trying to do more things in less time makes us more mindful, cultivates awareness and increases our appreciation of everything. Knowing and perceiving the reality of impermanence is not an excuse to live frivolously, insist always on the newest version of a series of strategically updated products, and ignore the dark cost of our recklessly disposable lifestyle. In an article "The Disposable Society: An Expensive Place to Live," writer Lisa Smith offers some ideas for turning our disposable age, with its built-in obsolescence, on its head, one rule-breaking individual/company at a time:[79]

- Practice voluntary simplicity

- Resist style-driven purchases/product generation

- Recycle

- Grow your own garden

- Be green at home, work, and in-between

- Bicycle, car-pool, take public transportation

- Downsize everything

- Start now

Remember, a turtle carries its home on its back. That's about as downsized as it gets. And because we create for what we hope someday will be a population of turtles, we must be sure to design products and services that embody true artisanship, reflect real value, and are made to last.

The Why for Because of It All

Just as individuals benefit from taking the time to discern their personal purpose and aspirations, companies can also find value in setting aside time to identify their purpose and vision.

That way, whatever mission, values, goals, and initiatives are adopted internally, they can then be manifested externally for customers. Strategies can be set in motion, and team members can flag activities that do not align with a company's core values. Firms must also allow time for all the strategies to be executed and implemented, and to penetrate the entire organization.

Taking time to talk to customers, and to nurture those relationships with a phone call, an in-person meeting, or a handwritten note, are all integral to the process of intentionally slowing down and getting deeper to the "bone and marrow" of what we do and why. When we take time to connect, listen, and understand, we also are then pristinely primed to anticipate needs, serve with authenticity and commitment, and create what is meaningful and valued.

The professional service company KPMG hosts a video series titled

The Entrée on its website where business owners and leaders gather in New York City eateries to converse on selected topics. In one episode, the conversation revolved around building a business with purpose. One guest, Bruce Pfau, a partner at Advisory Human Capital Strategy & Culture Transformation, mentioned how President Kennedy once saw a man sweeping the floors at Cape Canaveral and asked him what it was he did. The man replied, "Why Mr. President, I am helping to put a man on the moon."[80]

Journalist and host Joie Chen talked about businesses being in touch with their "higher purpose." The guests at the table all agreed that when a business knows its purpose, when you tap into something deeper, you capture the hearts and minds of your people.[81] Claudia Saran, Principal, U.S. People & Change Advisory Lead, identified the pride that comes when companies have a higher purpose. Employees are motivated and engaged, are more productive, and become ambassadors of the company and its products. The higher purpose transcends any statement that comes out of the boardroom, and becomes a driver that employees feel in complete accord with and can put in their own words. When people see, live, and breathe the message, it becomes a part of them and becomes a part of the culture. People begin to feel like they are a part of the plan, a part of the story of the company which is made up of all the stories of all those who work toward "the purpose."[82] According to *The Entree*, 73% of purpose-oriented people are satisfied in their jobs. When a company is authentically working toward a good cause, productivity increases up to 30%. People make extra efforts and go the extra mile knowing they are creating something meaningful and valued.[83]

In 2015, I met Shilpa Shah at the Forbes Women's Summit. Shilpa and Karla Gallardo are founders of the online fashion brand Cuyana, which creates premium essentials for today's woman. One of the unique aspects of Cuyana is that it encourages women to really curate the contents of their closets and to pare their wardrobe contents down to just a few essentials that they actually really love and that have meaning in their lives. Along with its emphasis that "less is more," the exclusively online Cuyana provides customers with the story behind each product's creation, from the region of the world it came from to the manufacturing process that brought it to life. The brand identifies as being "farm-to-table," but from a fashion perspective. Whether it's textiles from Turkey or jewelry from Peru, the Cuyana website provides e-commerce transparency, letting visitors browse the regions from where its products herald.[84]

Shah and her business partner realized that, while they had been selling mostly to people they knew, they were not achieving growth through the word-of-mouth advertising that they needed. They delved into their marketing strategy and discovered that they had neglected to give their "friends and family" customers the right messages with which to pitch the company's unique narrative and qualities. Their brand essence of making thoughtful, intentional choices was getting diluted.[85]

Shah and Gallardo hired a consulting firm to help them craft their tagline: "Fewer, Better Things." It took 18 months. But a memorable tagline that quickly communicates the value of your brand is attractive to investors. To customers, the tagline suggests a philosophy and way of living. Cuyana targets millennial consumers who care about owning products that have meaning. In 2013, Cuyana raised $1.7 million in funding when it launched. In spring of 2014, the San Francisco-based startup had grown 10 times larger, with more than 20 full-time employees plus contractors. Clearly, their tagline and logo, as streamlined as the closets they seek for their products, delivered the "why-for-because" of their brand in a compelling and memorable way.[86]

Recently, I came across an article written by Natasha Lampard in *The Pastry Box Project* that discusses the oldest company in the world, Nishiyama Onsen Keiunkan, established in 705 AD. This traditional Japanese hot spring hotel, located in the southern alps of Japan's Yamanashi Prefecture, is in its 52nd generation of continuous family management. According to Lampard, everything about this "onsen" is impeccable, from its 24/7 operation, to its ultrapure water, to its fresh and artfully prepared meals, to its humble and exemplary hospitality. The onsen is a temple of tranquility and the focus of its staff is on the continuation and quality experience of the onsen, not their own personal goals and gain.[87]

Most firms have some idea of how long they intend to remain in business. For some, longevity of an undetermined period of time is desired. Others are attracted to the new world model of building a company up to a point where it becomes a viable candidate for merger or acquisition. In her article, Lampard offered what she perceives as the distinctive choices available to today's entrepreneur:

- Focus on either the bottom or top line,

- Revolve around raising funds and exiting, or

- Achieve goals quickly and cheaply.

We can craft our businesses with an endpoint, an "exit strategy," in mind. We also have the option of attending to every minute detail, providing relentlessly exceptional service, and focusing on an "exist" strategy. In her exposé on Nishiyama Onsen Keiunkan, Lampard discussed *omotenashi,* the spirit of selfless service, humble hospitality, and the desire to personalize customer experience and exceed all expectations. This notable Japanese concept of wholehearted hospitality

dictates that a service provider abandon all self-interest and strive to anticipate every possible need a customer or guest may have. The utmost attention is paid to every detail and the best possible service is provided without expectation of reward. *Omotenashi* may have its origins in the traditional Japanese tea ceremony.[88]

The spirit of this practice transforms simple entrepreneurial undertakings into what Lampard calls "longtrepreneurial thinking."[89] It constitutes the difference between simply providing a service versus providing an exquisitely crafted experience. When entrepreneurial becomes "longtrepreneurial," businesses blossom. Dedication and passion nurture the very roots of a business. Such careful tending garners loyalty and appreciation. As word of mouth becomes legacy, hope or expectation of longevity also evolves. Brand loyalty can inspire a continuing tradition of exceptional quality across years, decades and maybe even centuries. The proof of what great love, care, and crafting can do is right there in businesses like Nishiyama Onsen Keiunkan, which has stayed the hand of impermanence, and achieved a sort of immortality.

Perhaps the practice of mindful existence, dedication to core principles, commitment to serving customers, and continuous crafting of meaningful products and services become the straw through which businesses may sip the elixir of immortality. If businesses can practice an economy of resources, nurturing and developing even that which is small and meaningful without overreaching and extending beyond what is truly manageable or even necessary, a great crafted experience can evolve. In other words, if a business contains its energy in a smaller footprint and constantly attends to cultivating and perfecting every detail of that footprint, it will ultimately transform from a simple business and service to a legendary experience forged with passion and embodying high art.

Be the turtle. Attend passionately and deliberately to what you know and what you are creating. Maintain stability by being careful not to extend too far beyond the footprint of the shell. Proceed at a pace that is comfortable and appropriate. Understand that the shell represents an "exist" strategy. There is no exiting. Move ever forward. Define and embrace what is meaningful, and stay true to your values and purpose. Develop, recognize and acknowledge your support systems (sometimes people do stop and help turtles across the road). Know your limits, polish your skills, and gravitate toward doing that which you love, that which is in your nature. Look, listen and perceive, and once in a while, just linger peacefully, stretched out on that log in the sun.

Case Study: Enrico Cuini

Enrico Cuini plumbs the depths of every discipline and distraction that arrests his attention. Fueled by an insatiable thirst for knowledge, this modern *Vitruvian Man* has delved into the worlds of art, engineering, chemistry, philosophy, physics, biology, history, architecture, and photography. He is a person of embracing expansion, focused on better understanding how the world, in all its mystery, works. He is a man composed of earth, metal, air, fire and water who knows he is both a microcosm of the universe and a part of the all. His awareness of the physical, mental, and spiritual levels enables him to see and feel naturally and deeply. Enrico understands action, connection and impact, and the importance of being absolutely present to whatever is before him in the Now.

When he was a boy, Enrico accompanied his father, who had an architecture and construction business, to trade conventions. He worked long hours among passionate people of artistic, technical and learned, professional backgrounds. Whereas many children aged 10 would be busy playing, Enrico's industrious childhood sculpted him with discipline, a superior work ethic, a curiosity about the intricacies of all things, a love of knowledge, and the energy of inspiration. Working 28 consecutive years at the Cersaie of Bologna and the Milan Salon of Design honed his artistic sensibilities and helped forge his destiny as an innovator and design leader.

Confident and enthusiastic, Enrico began expressing his artistic ideas at an early age. At 19 years old, he served as artistic director for the renowned club Paradiso in Rimini, where he created unique, high-profile events designed to entertain guests. Athletic by nature and deeply connected to the natural world, Enrico enjoyed competing in a variety of sports events. He felt a deep spiritual connection and kinship to water, which began at a young age. As a teenager, he became a European junior windsurfing champion and even tried out for a spot on the Olympic team. He also sailed and skied on the national circuit, played water polo and loved diving.

Fascinated with the world of proportions and properties, Enrico explores the alchemy of design and the natural sciences to create innovative and best-selling products and prototypes. He employs all his knowledge and experience gained through working with materials in the construction, nautical and sports worlds. Enrico likes working with his hands and feeling connected to the unformed matter and its potential. He understands the properties of elements and materials and how they react and act upon one another, and impact outcomes. With his knowledge from working with surfboards, boats, and for a flooring company, he developed new resins for flooring. When he was challenged with the assertion that there was nothing new to create in the lighting world, he developed a new lighting system. Enrico likes to problem solve. He loves to be of service, bringing his unique, broad spectrum of capabilities to the table and caring to create functional solutions.

As an innovator, entrepreneur, and designer, Enrico has elevated his childhood obsession with shoes into a quest to create the world's best footwear from a fashion, comfort, and environmentally responsible perspective. His commitment to his shoe craft begins at an almost elemental level, where he starts by having a meaningful conversation with the materials he will use. He considers the material, the feet, and the design as a whole, and creates collections of pure poetry.

Enrico's "Wing Shoes" project with orthopedic surgeon-turned-shoe-designer Dr. Taryn Rose is inspired by the airy lightness of butterfly wings. The shoes are designed to lift and support a woman's foot. His patented invention is being developed for DRESR, an innovative e-commerce platform founded by Taryn Rose. Enrico has channeled his knowledge of multiple disciplines into the creation of a new insole system. He has applied the architectural concept of tensegrity in the construction of a more stable, balanced and supportive shoe. His hands-on crafting of rich detail allows him to imbue his work more directly with his energy and to grace the feet of women everywhere with his artistic interpretations.

While he speaks English, French, and Italian, Enrico feels that the best communication happens when you view everyone as special and as a designer in their own right. Though humble about his education and accomplishments, Enrico is outspoken about his Enrico Cuini Foundation, a not-for-profit organization that partners innovation and commerce with philanthropy. He is committed to his vision where people all over the world have clean water, the freedom of expression that comes through education in the arts and design, and good healthcare. There is indeed a *Vitruvian Man* holism about Enrico. His painstaking devotion to every important detail of being, doing, and manifesting demonstrates how careful crafting of oneself can trickle down to meaningful crafting of positive change in the world.

Summary: Be the Turtle

Throughout time, people have sought magical elixirs and fountains of youth to extend their lives, and thus their stories. Creatives yearn for the longevity of what they craft into being. In an age when most purchases get discarded within two years, the challenge is to innovate products, brands and services that endure.

Our throwaway society designs with inherent obsolescence. People now display an institutionalized addiction to craving the next iteration of a product or brand. This brand brainwashing offers the antithesis of craftsmanship. My own mother faced this dilemma in her fine furniture store. She wrestled against the fast and cheap value system that promoted lesser quality products at a cheaper price. Our disposable consumer mindset is environmentally toxic and an unconscionable waste of precious and rapidly depleting natural resources.

It is time to incorporate, on a systemic level, a durable goods society that expands quality of life beyond just a financial focus. With a projected world population of over 8 billion people by 2020, we cannot continue to mass-produce and throw away. In order to slow the pace of climate change and reverse all our other negative impact on the planet, we must become rule breakers of the most mindful order. Here are some revolutionary ideas:

- Practice voluntary simplicity

- Resist style-driven purchases/product generation

- Recycle

- Grow your own garden

- Be green at home, work, and in-between

- Bicycle, car-pool, take public transportation

- Downsize everything

- Start now

At both a personal and professional level, it is time to slow down and dig deep into the marrow of what we do and why. It is time to take a measure of ourselves. Are we primed to anticipate needs, serve with authenticity and commitment, and create what is meaningful and valued?

A hotel in Japan that is now in its 52nd generation of family management can hold some valuable lessons for us. It is run according to the Japanese concept of *omotenashi,* the spirit of selfless service, humble hospitality, and the desire to personalize customer experience and exceed all expectations. The spirit of this practice transforms entrepreneurial undertakings into long-lived traditions. Dedication, great attention to detail and passion garner loyalty and appreciation, which translates into a kind of immortality.

Perhaps mindfulness, dedication to principles, commitment to customers, and the crafting of meaningful products and services will become the straw through which creatives, brands and businesses may sip the elixir of immortality. Be the turtle. Move at a comfortable pace. Define what is meaningful. Be authentic, champion integrity and stay true to your values and purpose.

10 *Winning the Big Race*

It's Time

Throughout these last couple of years, during the course of writing this book, I have spoken to brand leaders, craftsmen, educators, inventors, students, entrepreneurs, musicians, executives, healers, chefs, and everyday people. I repeatedly heard people voicing the same message aloud: It's about time that someone writes about slowing this frenetic pace of life down. We need someone to challenge this crazy need for speed, and question the velocity of this digital technology age, or at least the degree to which we participate in it.

It is evident that this resistance to rapid momentum is something that is in people's hearts and on their minds, but no one has quite known how or been courageous enough to voice their dissent without seeming obstructive, adverse or archaic. It is as if they fear risking their jobs, the success of their companies, or ridicule by coworkers, clients or peers by expressing their concerns against the scrum, the agile, the lean, the fast, and the epidemic of rapid prototyping. But in their hearts, they know they are exhausted, and their nervous systems are rattled and fraying. They are tired of the rat race, and tired of having to constantly "check in" to stay relevant, cool, and competitive. It is clear they feel as if they have no control over time, or their own future.

Sometimes it takes great loss, tragedy or life-threatening illness for us to realize the extreme fragility and brevity of our lives. We are only here in this moment. I like to think that we are here to do as much as we can with great love and authenticity. Our actions will be our legacy and will determine how we will be remembered. Often during these last couple of years I've seen some timely buzzwords popping up on design agency websites, marketing campaigns, and in the media: mindfulness, intention, craft, artisanship, meaning, happiness, passion, and love. The very concepts and practices I have been writing earnestly about are working their way into mainstream culture. It is their time to be explored, and it is our time to recognize them as tools for enriching every aspect of our lives. Even Morgan Spurlock made a movie called *Crafted*. It is no accident that this mindset is making its public appearance now.

We are at a tipping point where technology is poised to run away with our lives. I believe that people are trying to find their voice, to speak up and show the world the importance of slowing down, being more in the moment, and bringing life into balance. People crave the opportunity to appreciate process, synchronistic occurrences, and the art of creating something with their hands. They are cognizant, in heart and mind, of the need to occasionally challenge the trends of technology and the crazy cycle of life we are caught in and from which we need to pause and catch our breath.

This book project has connected us to both the like-minded with whom our observations resonate and the naysayers who readily challenge our thought processes and our philosophy. But as we embarked on this journey to find other closet artisans and craftspeople, other Turtles, we built strong case studies, illustrating that this slower, more thoughtful process can in fact be scaled and applied across industries, platforms, and cultures. By initiating the conversation, we believe that rabbits will grow more comfortable just hopping thoughtfully and maybe trying on a shell, and turtles may find moments when it is wise to plod a little faster.

Hopefully, as you read this book, you noticed that you were breathing easier, that your heart rate had slowed, your blood pressure stabilized, and your spirit felt strangely buoyed and uplifted at being reassured at last that you are not alone in your desire for a simpler (slower), more sane and sustainable way of living, crafting, and serving. Through the content of this book, I hope I was able to help you separate signals from noise, refocus, and channel your energy to something that is meaningful to you. Of course, it may also be that I simply stirred the mud at the bottom of the pond and you are more confused than ever about what you should be doing and how (fast) you should be doing it. You may feel that my message greatly resonates with your heart and your natural pace, but you have no obvious and safe way to jump off the carousel spinning faster than your equilibrium can stand it. That's okay. Sit with it all (like a turtle would), and you are certain to gain new insights and eventually an approach that feels appropriate to you.

Across these many pages, I've discussed a framework for design, entrepreneurship and basically any and all endeavor. This framework consists of purpose, meaning, innovation, business, value, time, and money. I've explored rational approaches, heart-centered approaches, prime motivators and meaning, and the real crux of the matter: the interconnectedness and interdependency between individuals, societies, cultures, business, and the environment. I also talked about finding love and happiness and how those drivers feed our individual souls and our collective neighborhood, community, and global spirit.

Through all the discussion, I brought us to the realization that there is no single solution for all cases and scenarios. And not everything is about the bottom line—money. The focus of every creative endeavor is people, their quality of life, and the creation of healthy, beautiful and sustainable environments in which all of life on this planet can thrive. Business is very personal. We're not just dealing with facts, figures, strategies, approaches, processes, deliverables, and outcomes. Our focus is not simply about how quickly or expeditiously we can go from concept and ideation to creation and implementation. Business, and how we conduct it, impacts us individually, socially, economically, culturally, and environmentally. A deep awareness of this ripple effect of every thought and action cultivates a powerful sense of responsibility and sensitivity. It requires us to move from our reactive state of impulsivity so common in our light-speed lifestyles, to a more considered and mindful state that allows us to ponder best approaches and optimal outcomes. By taking time to really think and appreciate, we also have greater opportunity to communicate and collaborate for more broadly beneficial results.

> Business, and how we conduct it, impacts us individually, socially, economically, culturally, and environmentally.

Interpretations of the story of the tortoise and the hare and the lessons implied in the famous fable continue to be explored and expanded for relevance in this challenging age. In one version on YouTube, the tortoise and the hare take turns winning and losing the race. After each loss, the loser takes time to evaluate the situation and discover, with new eyes, new approaches that deliver more excellent outcomes. Ultimately, the two competitors dialogue with one another, devise a strategy that utilizes each of their core competencies and decide on a course of action where everyone wins.[90]

This book is the equivalent of that dialogue between the tortoise and the hare. It is a guide, with illustrations, checkpoints and reminders that we must balance our need for speed and our tendency toward myopic focus with essential mindfulness around creative endeavor. If we are designing and delivering tangible products and services that will have use and appeal today, let us also consider their place and purpose beyond the immediate and into tomorrow. We live in an age of dwindling resources and increasing demand for them. Our imagination around our creations must also stretch into the future. When we understand our responsibility to be good stewards of all that we touch, we understand in a deeper way our connection to everything and everyone, everywhere.

Yes, we are all connected in more ways than we can even imagine or anticipate. No longer do we have to travel in tall ships and journey for months at the mercy of wind, rain, and engulfing wave to get to another land. We travel thousands of miles physically in just a few hours, or the same distance virtually in just a few seconds. Our impact and influence on landscape, resources, climate and habitable environments is immediate and indelible. Our effect on one another's lives, cultures and homelands is not merely serendipitous; it does not happen simply by chance or blind luck. The reality of our connected world binds us together; therefore, it is both prudent and responsible to be measured and mindful in our actions, conscious of our craftsmanship, and forward thinking in our creative works. If we blend hare happenstance with turtle temperateness and consistency, we can open our eyes and trace the patterns and probable outcomes of our most synchronistic dance together.

Serendipity and Synchronicity in Creativity: Putting It All Together

What are the roles of synchronicity and serendipity in the creative process and in our work and lives in general? Great, meaningful, and award-winning creative effort is typically born of passionate commitment, focused intensity, and hard work. As a designer, I know that when I direct my attention toward a design challenge, set my goals, generate ideas, and commit to a vision, then observations and occurrences related to the challenge begin to occur.

Now, whenever something beneficial happens unexpectedly and by pure luck or chance, it is coined "serendipity"—viewed as a serendipitous event. But as creatives, we can't rely on impulse and moments of blind luck to execute our vision and bring our ideas forward. Blind luck is merely a sign that we are disconnected from awareness and do not have our intuitive eyes open to discern the relatedness of where we've been, where we find ourselves currently, and how we will get where we wish to go. In making meaningful connections, we dash less and deliberate more. Thoughtful awareness guides our consideration.

In the design world where I live, I focus hard on my work, research extensively, field ideas, and seek answers. This tasks my brain to make new connections. I delegate to my senses the assignment of sifting through all the stimuli surrounding me in order to zero in on what is most relevant and beneficial to my current cause. In this fertile field of focused intention, synchronicity, or "meaningful coincidences" (a term identified by Swiss Psychologist Carl Gustav Jung) happens.[91]

We've all had the experience of finding something new and novel that we like—whether it's a particular model car, a hand bag, or a lawn ornament—and then suddenly seeing that new object of our interest everywhere. Our fascination activates our inner detective; our focus opens up our awareness, sharpens our perceptions, and heightens our ability to discern and distill relevant information and make connections. When we are aware and mindful, we are open to the rhythms of our journey, operating purposefully, watchful for the signs that we are on the right course, and in tune with the creative forces that exist within the world and ourselves.

As the CEO of my own companies, I live and work in awe of the synchronicities that pepper the landscape of my interactions with projects and people. I work mindfully, with my eyes open to infinite potential, gauging clues, taking nothing for granted, and leaving no stone unturned as I ply my craft. I believe that there are no "coincidences," and realize that everyone I meet has something to share with me or teach me. I meet unusual suspects in off-the-beat places with a seemingly random collision of ideas and interests, and realize we have creative work to do together. I go to conferences and discover that the knowledge I share with others has the potential to make a good book. I engage creativity and the discovery process and find myself looking at project challenges in a new way. And so I follow the threads, the bread crumbs that highlight the trail to discovery, and mine the riches the universe intends for me if I only have eyes to see. Most of all, I reside in gratitude for the gift of awareness.

I have been graced with more synchronicities in my life than I can count, but for purposes of illustration within the pages of this text, I will share a few that stand out. Approximately 10 years ago, my family and I patronized a Chinese restaurant during the busiest time of the year, on the Chinese New Year reunion dinner night. Because seating was at such a premium, and every seat in the house needed to be filled, we were asked to share a table with strangers. It became quickly apparent that I had much in common with my new tablemates on both a philosophical, business, and personal level. We stayed connected following that dinner and became friends. These new friends then became clients of mine, and now our kids celebrate birthdays and holidays together.

Another example of synchronicity occurred when I spent my own money and hosted the movie *Design & Thinking* (a movie which explores how people are changing the world with their creative thinking and collaboration) for the design community in San Diego.[92] I brought the movie's producer, Yuhsiu Yang, to San Diego for the screening and discussion afterwards, and gave him all the proceeds from the ticket sales. My motivation in all of that was simply to start a conversation among creatives. I was not seeking any sort of monetary gain, recognition or notoriety. But suddenly two months later, I found myself in Taiwan where I attended and hosted a workshop on Design Thinking.

That amazing and meaningful synchronicity happened because there was purity of intention, positive energy, and desire for beneficial outcomes for everyone. I am a big believer in "karma." Synchronicity came into play because out of my passion for my craft and my genuine desire to make a positive difference in my profession, my community (world and otherwise) and life, I'd set in motion the momentum for meaningful and related opportunities to occur.

Tony Robbins has described how potential resources suddenly make themselves available to people focused determinedly on a vision or goal. He said, "Once you decide that something is a priority, you give it tremendous emotional intensity, and by continually focusing on it, any resource that supports its attainment will eventually become clear."[93] The field of energy and conscious awareness you weave around your goal automatically sets up a chain of beneficial events with no visible connection that help unwrap its potential and expand its possibilities of discovery and achievement. The more you become aware, the more the synched occurrences seem to manifest. We become connected with a river of infinite possibilities. It is almost as if the Universe is listening and we have only to ask and focus.

Crossing the Finish Line

It was synchronicity again that gave me the good fortune to meet and get to know Amanda North, founder of Artisan Connect, former VP of Marketing for Splunk, and Boston Marathon bombing survivor. Originally, I was researching competitors for my client Varonis. Amanda once held the same position at Splunk that my client David holds at Varonis. I wanted to get to know her better and make some comparisons. It turned out that she was friends with my friend Ellen Petry Leanse, so Ellen introduced us. Amanda and I talked at length. She eventually shared

> The more you become aware, the more the synched occurrences seem to manifest. We become connected with a river of infinite possibilities. It is almost as if the Universe is listening and we have only to ask and focus.

with me her very personal story of awakening to a life filled with passion and purpose following the marathon bombing horror, and her inspiration became the wrap up for this book. This 30-year tech industry veteran recognized the gift she'd been given in having her life spared during the bombing, and decided to risk everything, break the rules, and craft a life that had meaning and could impact other lives all around the globe in positive ways.

At the time of the bombing, Amanda was VP of Marketing for AOptix in Campbell, California. She went to Boston to watch her daughter run the marathon and to cheer her on. Little did Amanda realize that she was 10 feet away from the first bomb when it detonated. Shaken and confused, Amanda attended an injured woman near her, not realizing that she herself had shrapnel injuries, burns, and lacerations. Life would never be the same for Amanda and her daughter Lili. The realization that a person's world could change or end in an instant caused her to re-evaluate her life and all that she stood for, felt passionate about, found wondrous and inspiring, and loved to do. The national tragedy that had ripped so explosively through so many lives had caused a new woman to emerge from the smoke and screams and confusion. Amanda turned away from the virtual world of software launches and updates and became immersed in the world of the tangible, founding a startup that makes a difference in the lives of artisans from developing countries.[94]

Artisan Connect is an online marketplace where collective and non-profit artisan groups can sell the craft wares of individual artisans globally, and artisans can be assured of a sustainable, fair wage in return. You can read more about Amanda's story in the case study accompanying this chapter. She is an inspiring example of the power of One, and the difference a single person can make in the lives of many if they simply step back, re-evaluate priorities, listen to their inner voice, pay attention to their core interests and competencies, and follow their hearts. When you are "in synch" with yourself, synchronicities appear around you to add momentum to achieving your dreams. For Amanda, a race marred by tragedy inspired a whole new set of meaningful goals to achieve and significant finish lines in life to cross.

Being a craftsperson and mastering your turtle nature will mean something different to each person who reads and is inspired by this book. What does becoming a Turtle Master mean? It might mean any of the following:

- You make deliberate efforts to introduce craft and add value into everything you do.

- You take time to ideate and develop additional concepts in order to create products and services that are optimal, reliable, sustainable, and have longevity.

- You define success as exploring solutions that improve the lives of people globally, or even the life of just one person.

- You keep your business small and simple, and work diligently every day to improve upon yesterday, and to keep your employees and customers happy.

- You attend, with precision and care, to the smallest detail of a project, no matter how seemingly unimportant.

People ask me if I think that I am a Turtle Master. The answer is "no," or at least "not yet." Maybe instead I identify more with world-renowned sushi chef Master Jiro, who is in daily pursuit of making the best sushi in the world. Even though the world has bestowed upon him his three Michelin stars, he continues to discover new and better ways of making the best sushi. For the true Turtle Master, the finish line never really comes because the work is never done. Perfection is always an ideal, and its achievement is only an approximation. There are always ways to improve upon everything, no matter how skilled, how expert, how exquisite the product. And so the true craftsperson, the Turtle Master, finds joy and satisfaction in the daily practice (dare I say meditation) of plying his or her craft.

Sense and Sensibility

I have been labeled as being driven, tenacious, ambitious, insatiable, relentless, unwavering, determined, zealous, passionate, and the list goes on. Sometimes that is just someone else's way of telling me that they don't want to be near me because I am "wired." Regardless of the label, deep down in my heart, my justification for however I am being perceived is that I simply care to refine my designer's sixth sense. I strive to employ all my senses in my work—my intuition, instinct, intellect, sight, smell, taste, hearing, equilibrium, sense of touch, and moral sense—in order to detect subtleties, and channel that energy to bring out the best in others. German philosopher Immanuel Kant once said, "All our knowledge begins with the senses, proceeds then to the understanding, and ends with reason."[95]

We all have this extra sense, which some refer to as our sixth sense. Talking about that "extra sense receptor," or extra sensory perception is like me telling everyone that there is a Buddha alive in them. It's not something you encounter in daily conversation. It can be controversial, and some might not find it appropriate for a professional sphere. Some might even consider it absurd or offensive. But the new science of quantum healing would support the supposition and then some. It is not the extraordinary ability of a gifted few. It exists within each of us and can be developed and enhanced through mindfulness practices.

Our five senses interpret the energy data around us. Everything that exists is energy, is infused with consciousness, and has a particular vibration and resonance. We exist, quite literally, in a river of information. Our sixth sense is our internal navigator. It senses things that are still waves of probability, and guides us along the path toward making our dreams and heart's desires tangible. With all the external noise in our environment, with the deluge of messages coming at us from every angle every minute of every day, it can be quite challenging to listen to that interior voice and really receive the guidance it offers. The distractions around us deafen, intrude, and energetically drain us. For that reason, we must engage a practical aesthetic that will expand our consciousness, sharpen our focus and rewire our brains. Each of us must take time regularly to quiet our beings, still our minds, and meditate. It is important to go within our shells, to "be" with our dreams, passions, and inspirations, and then find a way to bring that song of ourselves, the music of our true creative essence, fully into the world. When we can touch the core of our being, and can perceive and follow that light within, we will find ourselves living our purpose. There is no greater or more satisfying feeling in the world.

This turtle path of taking time to do something well, committing myself to my art, and being sensitive to every detail, even the minor ones, is the path that I have chosen. I walk and live it. And although this pursuit of perfection for the purpose of delivering authentic value and enhancing a global quality of life may not be for the faint hearted, there are actually many amazing people out there who believe in and also live this path. There's Vicky Tsai of Tatcha fame, Amanda North, and all the other Turtle Masters featured in the case studies contained within these pages. These inspiring entrepreneurs have taken their passion and dreams and built great businesses and become community leaders, all the while advocating the core values of true artisans and craftspeople. I aspire to be like them. They give me hope and lift my spirit. They make the world a better place for all of us.

Perhaps you too will find that this book has struck a chord somewhere deep within you. We hope you will join us by excavating and unleashing all the creative potential and passion for your craft that is within you. We invite you to help grow this movement, this evolution of excellence through mindful exploration of your own passions and motivations, and the careful application of craft in all you do. We would love to hear from you and invite your feedback and your stories as together we craft a collaborative world of great beauty, health, compassion, integrity, inspiration, originality, delight, wonder and wholeness. We have the tools and the power, and hopefully we have the vision, will and determination. So, are you ready? On your mark, get set, let's go!

Case Study: Amanda North, CEO of Artisan Connect

Amanda North is a modern-day Renaissance woman. Having earned her BA in politics and economics from Princeton University and her MBA from Stanford University, she spent the next 30 years in the tech industry. Amanda served as Vice President of Marketing and Corporate Communications for several globally focused firms. She ran the Desktop Publishing Group at Apple, is a private pilot, is a mentor at Santa Clara University's Global Social Benefits Institute, serves on the steering committee of the Alliance for Artisan Enterprise, is a trustee of *Business Today* magazine, and sits on the board of Sustainable Travel International. After being injured in the Boston Marathon bombing and witnessing the horror of that day, Amanda underwent a transformation, renewing her commitment to pursuing her passions. Shortly thereafter, she founded Artisan Connect, which provides artisans in developing countries with market access for their home décor products.

According to Amanda, investors look for founders whose motivation in starting a new company goes beyond any financial incentive. She always harbored a latent desire to make a global impact. She was raised that way, and her great education helped tool her skills for making a difference in the world. When she started out at Apple in the 1980s, she helped implement technology that enabled others to achieve global impact. It was what Apple stood for, and there was practically a missionary zeal. Amanda loved it.

She was a single mom raising two kids and working to keep a roof over their heads. She did what she had to do, but always felt somehow that she wasn't doing enough. Then came the terrorist bombing at the Boston Marathon on April 15, 2013. There to support her daughter who was running the race, Amanda got caught in the worst of the devastation as she stood a mere 10 feet from the first explosion. That night in the hospital, when she and her daughter reconnected after a full day of not knowing what had happened to the other, her daughter said, "Mom, we've been spared by a miracle. Our lives will never be the same. We must focus on our passion and purpose." It was a very moving experience. That was her spark. Amanda could no longer put her passion on hold. She realized that one never knows what will happen next. She felt called to focus her energies on the things that matter. Amanda spent time discerning where she could make a difference and realized that for her it was always about traveling to places that are in danger of somehow disappearing and beyond.

During her travels, she discussed with artisans that they could very well be the last in their generation and culture doing what they've been doing. Because they have not been paid fairly, many have disrupted their way of life, and given up their craft in order to pursue higher paying jobs. What Amanda heard in her discussions with artisans was that they needed market access to people who would really value what they were doing, and who would understand some of the issues in production, and what it's like to live in the developing world. This literally became the concept for Artisan Connect: Sustaining Developing World Artisans with Market Access.

Amanda learned a great deal along the way about the difference between working in the technology industry versus retail and its engagement of the entire ecosystem. The supply chain is a really important part of this as there is much involved in getting products to market. In tech you have software launches, and those can happen on an evolving basis. A decade ago there were one to two major software updates a year. Now it's continual. Because software is fungible, you can do it anywhere in the world and it is completely transparent because bits move at almost the speed of light. But Artisan Connect deals with physical items that are handmade individually. They are affected by a lot of externalities. For example, there are artisans working in the highlands of Cusco, Peru, an area that cannot be physically accessed during periods of heavy snowfall. Or there are parts of the world that celebrate long religious holidays such as Ramadan, where nothing else goes on. All of this must be taken into account in the work schedule. There are times of bad weather, like typhoons, that can devastate production schedules because either supplies go away or the artisans have to attend to things like rebuilding their homes.

In some respects, Amanda feels that her work is almost like a cultural exchange mission. Artisan Connect is building a community of people who are passionate about sustaining artisans around the world. The company focused on home décor after examining existing artisan efforts and how people like to shop. Jewelry and fashion sectors already exist, but home décor is pretty open. So Artisan Connect began with that as a focus as it seemed to be better from a consumer standpoint. People like knowing what they are going to find within a certain sector, and it provides a revenue stream for the artisans. Artisan Connect has a broader mission—engagement: travel, storytelling, having people outside of the organization's staff telling stories about traveling and meeting the artisans.

Product making can be very complex, and Artisan Connect strives to deliver that story to customers. The organization wants its public to have an immersive experience, as if they are interacting directly with the artisans. One of the big pushes involves having artisan groups take iPhone videos of their production process which may not be of high production quality, but they show how the products are made. Artisan Connect also tells stories about the cultures and places it works through blogs. This gives people a window into not just how the products are made, but also the lives of the people and the geography of the area that is sourced. Storytelling is a big part of what makes Artisan Connect unique and special and it's an important part of helping the organization build its assets.

It is key to build connections between artisans and their markets in a way that is not ethnocentric. We all know that one almost has to live in a culture to understand its cultural nuances and taboos. Artisan Connect encourages customers and potential visitors to have an open mind in order to properly experience another culture. Engagement through storytelling helps break down the barriers. In many countries, such as Burma (which is very poor), people look healthy and well-taken care of. Part of this may be due to the fact that everything is still community driven. People take care of each other. They have their ways of existence, which may include their own pocket farm where they can grow vegetables. And yes, there are squat toilets. Even though people are not making a lot of money, they are enriched by their community, by their deeply spiritual way of life, and by their intrinsic sense of feeling they are part of a whole.

Ultimately, Artisan Connect wants to be a lifestyle company that delivers on people's desire for high quality, beautiful products that they love, and on their desire for meaningful purchases that have social impact. Artisan Connect wants to be a very successful company and brand that authentically means and stands for all of that. Through revenue generation and working through ethical sources, it wants to create a lot of different support systems for its artisans, including such things as health care, and education systems. Over time, it may provide training for artisans to help them thrive.

In Silicon Valley, one of the things people say explicitly is that with the fast pace of technology leading life, a person must have a connection back to something that reminds them of other lives, cultures, and ways of living. Having the symbolic representations of how others live within our personal space connects us to their stories. These crafted products provide linkage to areas of the world we might easily forget about and that are in danger of being lost. And as people connect with the products, they provide the important impact that supports artisans and preserves their craft, culture, and way of life.

Amanda North is hopeful about the future and the ability of people to connect in meaningful ways. Part of her dissatisfaction with Silicon Valley and its focus on competition and accumulating egregious wealth is the tiring and empty satisfaction of endless, self-serving competition. While she cares to have adequate funds to provide for her children, to live in comfortable circumstances and to travel, she is not motivated by excessive wealth. She is motivated by the opportunity to provide a paradigm for a type of company that enables people to thrive financially and have an inspiring place to work while treating everyone along the entire supply chain fairly, from the artisan suppliers to their investors.

Moving forward, Amanda is focused on forming a small, fantastic team and robust management team committed to the company's mission and who possess the deep skills and expertise to lead it forward. As her role as CEO becomes more defined, Amanda's attention is focused on HR and hiring, making sure the organization gets funded, and managing investors. She wants to make sure that she and her team remain deeply involved in the personal storytelling as far as possible, and that they continue to deliver that personal engagement. She sees great importance in periodically going out into the field to visit the artisans, to stay connected, and to witness the impact firsthand. Now that's passion.

Post Script: Since this interview was conducted, Artisan Connect merged with Nest--a non-profit organization headquartered in New York City that is building a new handworker economy to increase global workforce inclusivity, improve women's well-being beyond factories, and preserve important cultural traditions around the world. Amanda serves as an advisor to Nest.

Summary: Winning the Big Race

I often hear people voice discontent with the frenetic pace of the lives we now lead. People crave the opportunity to appreciate process, synchronistic occurrences, and the art of creating something with their hands. And yet, the thought of resisting this swift current makes them nervous or fearful. Our actions will be our legacy.

We are at a tipping point. Technology is running away with our lives. Throughout this book we have demonstrated the efficacy of slowing down and adopting a more natural pace. We have initiated the conversation of how mindfulness and thoughtful processes can in fact be scaled and applied across industries, platforms, and cultures.

If this message resonates with you, pursue it. If you are unsure, sit with the ideas, and perhaps experiment with our rational, heart-centered framework for mindfully crafting all aspects of living: purpose, meaning, innovation, value, time, etc. The focus of every creative endeavor is people, their quality of life, and the creation of healthy, beautiful and sustainable environments. Understanding the ripple effect of every thought and action cultivates a sense of responsibility and greater awareness of more broadly beneficial interactions with the world. Use this book to open the dialogue between the turtle and the hare that exist within you.

Change and discovering one's passion begins with whatever a person is authentically interested in. If it does not begin there, then starting any new business will just be too difficult. A person can look for great business opportunities, but if it's just cerebral and not heart based, it's not going to endure. The template for discernment is the thought process a person goes through when exploring their interests and discovering what they most gravitate towards. As an example, if the phone rings, do they take the call or not? What magazines do they subscribe to? How do they spend their vacations? These are "indicators." Self-assessment is also key. A person must be honest about their strengths, and what they have learned. Maybe they are fresh out of school without a lot of work experience but have a language major and multiple linguistic skills. Perhaps there is a region of the world that they care about a lot. Maybe they have a computer functional background that can be applied. Maybe they have a lot of experience but also other applicable skills such as fund raising, marketing, etc. It doesn't always take a life-changing experience for someone to gravitate towards doing something they love and feel "called" to do. And sometimes the universe does give them a nudge indicating their world is changing anyway, and it's time to explore what's in their heart and put it to practice.

Whatever a person's new endeavor may be, they must trust that there are a lot of support systems out there to help them. If they are assuming a new role, they may not know what those support systems are. It can be like parachuting into a new continent without any landmarks, and it's midnight, and they are without a compass or a flashlight. They feel all alone with no direction. But the fact of the matter is, there are a lot of organizations and people out there who have gone before them and documented their journey. It's important for the person to humbly acknowledge that they are coming in without a lot of experience. People will recognize this and want to help.

Each of us has experienced both serendipitous and synchronistic events. Pure serendipity, or lucky occurrences, cannot be depended upon to advance our vision or ideas. Synchronistic events, on the other hand, are meaningful coincidences that pepper the landscape of our interactions when we set our ideas in motion. Once you focus passionately on an ideal or a goal, the energy you weave around it automatically sets up a chain of beneficial events with no visible connection that help unwrap its potential and expand its possibilities. The more you become aware, the more the synched occurrences seem to manifest. If we really want a life that feels accessible, responsive, purposeful and satisfying, we must slow down enough to envision it. Sometimes the Universe detects that longing in our soul and will create events and circumstances that invite us to be true to ourselves.

If you are taking time to evaluate situations and discovering new approaches for more excellent outcomes, you may be unleashing your inner craftsperson and mastering your turtle nature. I have identified some indicators that reveal steps toward mastery:

- You strive to introduce craft and add value into everything you do.

- You take time to develop optimal, reliable, and enduring products and services.

- You define success as exploring solutions that improve lives.

- You keep business small and simple, and your employees and customers happy.

- You attend to the smallest detail of a project.

We are multi-sensory beings. Most of us are aware that we have five senses: sight, smell, taste, hearing and touch. Some of us are in touch with our sixth sense, our intuitive, insightful nature, which helps us detect subtleties. Our sixth sense is our internal navigator. It senses things that are still waves of probability, and guides us along the path toward making our dreams and heart's desires tangible. When we readily take time to quiet our beings, still our minds, and meditate, we actively develop our relationship with our sixth sense. We actively manifest our dreams.

The turtle path, the pursuit of craftsmanship for the purpose of delivering authentic value and enhancing a global quality of life, may not be for the faint hearted, but there are amazing people out there who live according to it. They have taken their passion and dreams and built great businesses and become community leaders. This book is an invitation to hear the calling within yourself and begin your mindful and purposeful journey. Together we can craft a collaborative world of great beauty, health, compassion, integrity, inspiration, originality, delight, wonder, and wholeness.

Postface

Mama: Can We Help You?

My kids love to draw—The moment they each turned two, I discovered that my boys were equally as "creative" as their mama. Evan, my oldest (now six), was always eager to build and make stuff, and Tyler (my three-year-old) loves to draw creatures holding hands.

For a while, their creative exploration absolutely didn't make any sense to me...until I developed my "turtle" patience: I became an observer. It all started with Evan dragging rolls and rolls of toilet paper all over the living room. And let me tell you, with the dog, an explosion of toys, and after a long day's work—all I wanted was a peaceful, CLEAN house. But this time, something stopped me from picking up after him. This time, I sat down, bit my tongue, and just gave out a big sigh and watched him—PLAY.

Something magical was unfolding right in front of me. He was tearing up toilet paper and arranging it as tracks for his little race cars. "Mama! Look—racetrack for my Lighting McQueen!" he belted out. And from then onwards, I never stopped my boys from having fun.

Today, my two boys are my biggest teachers. They teach me how to see the world in an "untainted" way: fresh, innocent, filled with joy, excitement, and as though all is still possible. They teach me patience. They teach me to laugh when the stress of single motherhood gets overwhelming. They gently remind me of the purpose of life, how to prioritize my time, and most importantly, how to do it all with joy.

So, as I embarked on this journey writing this book, I decided to include my boys in my creative process. They've inspired me to doodle with them, to express stories from a fresh perspective, and the visuals that accompany the stories are expressed in almost childlike vignettes, first sketched by my children and then finished in gouache by me.

This is a true collaborative effort between me and my children, almost three years in the making. I would not have been able to complete this book without their love and support.

Thank you Evan and Tyler. Mama loves you so much!

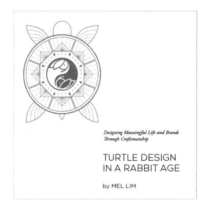

Notes

1. University Hospitals, UH Blog. "Top 5 Most Stressful Life Events" www.uhhospitals.org/myuhcare/health-and-wellness/better-living-health-articles/2015/july/the-top-5-most-stressful-life-events

2. Andrews, Ted. *Animal Speak: The Spiritual & Magical Powers of Creatures Great & Small* (Llewellyn Publications, Woodbury, Minnesota, First Edition, 35th Printing, 2007) Pg. 18

3. McAllister, Angela. *The Tortoise and the Hare: An Aesop's Fable* (Frances Lincoln Children's Books, 2nd edition, 2004)

4. Yannig. "Creativity Takes Time, Even in Online Co-Creation Contests" (eYeka, January 10, 2012) news.eyeka.net/2012/01/creativity-takes-time-even-in-online-co-creation-contests/

5. Breen, Bill. "The 6 Myths of Creativity" (*Fast Company,* December 2004) www.fastcompany.com/51559/6-myths-creativity

6. Sawyer.R. Keith. "The Hidden Secrets of the Creative Mind" (*TIME* January 16, 2006) content.time.com/time/magazine/article/0,9171,1147152,00.html

7. Kotchka, Claudia. "Claudia Kotchka on Innovation at P&G, Institute of Design Strategy Conference, May 2008" (IIT Institute of Design, May 2008) vimeo.com/5203345

8. Stinson, Elizabeth. "The Secret Sauce to a Mustang's Design is Still Clay and Tape" (*Wired,* April 17, 2014) www.wired.com/2014/04/the-secret-sauce-of-a-mustangs-design-is-still-clay-and-tape/

9. *Willy Wonka and the Chocolate Factory* (Paramount Pictures, 1971) Film adaptation of 1964 novel by Roald Dahl: *Charlie and the Chocolate Factory*)

10. Brandon, John. "Is Technology Making Us Less Human?" (*Techradar,* August 6, 2013) www.techradar.com/news/world-of-tech/future-tech/is-technology-making-us-less-human-1171002#article-body

11. McLuhan, Marshall. *Understanding Media: The Extension of Man* (Signet Books, 1964) Pg. 47

12. Koosel, Stacey. "Surfing the Digital Wave: Digital Identity as Extension" (McLuhan's Philosophy of Media Centennial Conference/Contact Forum 2011) www.academia.edu/2048738/Surfing-the-Digital-Wave-Digital-Identity-as-Extension

13. Brandon, John. "Is Technology Making Us Less Human?" (*Techradar,* August 6, 2013) www.techradar.com/news/world-of-tech/future-tech/is-technology-making-us-less-human-1171002#article-body

14. Knapton, Sarah. "Young People are 'Lost Generation' Who Can No Longer Fix Gadgets, Warns Professor" (*The Telegraph,* December 28, 2014) www.telegraph.co.uk/news/science/science-news/11298927/Young-people-are-lost-generation-who-can-no-longer-fix-gadgets-warns-professor.html

15. McSpadden, Kevin. "You Now Have a Shorter Attention Span Than a Goldfish" (*TIME,* May 14, 2015) www.time.com/3858309/attention-spans-goldfish/

16. Hibbard, Sheila. "Internet, Technology Fuels Our Lack of Patience" (*The Marketing Bit,* July 25, 2012) www.themarketingbit.com/infographics/internet-technology-fuels-our-lack-of-patience-infographic/

17. Alban, Deane. "The Cognitive Costs of Multitasking" (*Be Brain Fit*) https://bebrainfit.com/cognitive-costs-multitasking/

18. *The Meaning of Life* (Calendine Films, The Monty Python Partnership, Universal Pictures, UK; Starring John Cleese, Terry Gilliam, Eric Idle, and Terry Jones as Mr. Creosote; Released March 31, 1983)

19. Anxiety and Depression Association of America, August 2017. adaa.org/about-adaa/press-room/facts-statistics

20. Tolle, Eckhart. *The Power of Now: A Guide to Spiritual Enlightenment* (New World Library, Novato, CA, 1999) Pg. 59

21. Lokos, Allan. *Patience: The Art of Peaceful Living* (Penguin Group, USA; New York, 4th edition, January 2012)

22. Stritzel McCarthy, Cheryl. "Can Patience Co-Exist with Technology?" (*Chicago Tribune,* April 10, 2012) www.articles. chicagotribune.com/2012-04-10/features/sc-fam-0403-patience-technology-20120410_1_impatience-technology-young-people

23. Beliak, Julia. "Is Technology Making Our Lives Easier...Or Just Adding More Stress?" (*Huffington Post,* October 21, 2013) www.huffingtonpost.com/Julia-Beliak/womens-forum-2013_b_4138876.html

24. Clear, James. "40 Years of Stanford Research Found that People with This One Quality are More Likely to Succeed" (jamesclear. com, January 23, 2014) https://jamesclear.com/delayed-gratification

25. Crawford, Matthew. *Shop Class as Soul Craft: An Inquiry into the Value of Work* (The Penguin Press, New York, 2009) Pg. 20

26. *Jiro Dreams of Sushi* (Film documentary starring Jiro Ono; Magnolia Pictures; June 11, 2011)

27. Ebert, Roger. *Roger Ebert's Movie Yearbook 2013: 25th Anniversary Edition* (Andrew McMeel Publishing, Missouri, 2013) Pg. 306

28. Gladwell, Malcolm. *Outliers: The Story of Success* (Little, Brown & Co.; 2008)

29. *Dior and I.* (Film documentary; Paramount, September 1, 2015)

30. Sinek, Simon. *Start with Why: How Great Leaders Inspire Everyone to Take Action* (Portfolio; Reprint Edition; December 27, 2011)

31. Aristotle. Rhetorica I, 11.5; cited by Frijda, Nico: Manstead, Antony; Bem, Sasha. *The Influence of Emotions and Beliefs* (Cambridge University Press, 2000) Pg. 1

32. Seneca. De Ira, I, viii.1.

33. George Campbell, 1776, cited by Dillar, James Price; Meijnders, Anneloes. "Persuasion and the Structure of Affect," *The Persuasion Handbook* (Sage Publishing) Pg. 309

34. *Star Trek* (Desilu Productions, Norway Corp, Paramount Television, Desilu Studios, Culver City, CA) Released September 8, 1966

35. Childre, Doc Lew; Martin, Howard; Beech, Donna. *The HeartMath Solution: The Institute of HeartMath's Revolutionary Program for Engaging the Power of the Heart's Intelligence* (Harper One; Reprint Edition; August, 2000)

36. The Institute of HeartMath. "Accessing the Heart's Intuition: A Key to Global Coherence" (*Waking Times,* September 24, 2012) www.wakingtimes.com/2012/09/24/accessing-the-hearts-intuition-a-key-to-global-coherence

37. Harnish, Verne. *Scaling Up: How a Few Companies Make It...and Why the Rest Don't* (Rockefeller Habits 2.0) (*Gazelle's Inc;* 1st edition; October 21, 2014)

38. Kuraishi, Mari. Global Giving (www.globalgiving.org)

39. Alidina, Shamash; Marshall, Juelle Jane. "Cultivate Beginner's Mind for Mindfulness" (www.dummies.com) www.dummies.com/religion/spirituality/cultivate-beginners-mind-for-mindfulness/

40. Hanh, Thich Nhat. "Five Steps to Mindfulness" (*Mindful: Taking Time for What Matters,* August 23, 2010) www.mindful.org/five-steps-to-mindfulness/

41. Ibid.

42. Williams, Ray. "Is the Internet Making Us Dumber?" (*Psychology Today,* July 19, 2011) www.psychologytoday.com/blog/wired-success/201107/is-the-internet-making-us-dumber

43. "INSEAD Research Shows Mindfulness Meditation Linked to Better Decisions," February 10, 2014. *INSEAD: THE BUSINESS SCHOOL FOR THE WORLD.* www.insead.edu/news/2014-insead-wharton-meditation

44. Whitman, Walt. "Song of Myself" *Leaves of Grass: The First (1855) Edition* (Penguin, New York, 1986) Pg 54; Lines 647-648

45. Doidge, Norman. *The Brain's Way of Healing* (Penguin Books; Updated Edition; January 26, 2016) www.penguin.com/ajax/books/excerpt/9780670025503

46. Lieberman PhD., Dr. Matthew. "Why We Stop Learning: The Paradox of Expertise" (*Psychology Today,* June 19, 2012) www.psychologytoday.com/blog/social-brain-social-mind/201206/why-we-stop-learning-the-paradox-expertise

47. Ibid.

48. Rapp, Sarah. "Why Success Always Starts with Failure" (99U: Empowering the Creative Community) 99u.com/articles/7072/why-success-always-starts-with-failure

49. Watson-Smyth, Kate. "Secret History of Tupperware" (*Independent,* October 7, 2010) www.independent.co.uk/property/interiors/secret-history-of-tupperware-2100910.html

50. Wagner, Eric T. "Five Reasons 8 Out of 10 Businesses Fail" (*Forbes,* September 12, 2013) www.forbes.com/sites/ericwagner/2013/09/12/five-reasons-8-out-of-10-businesses-fail/#305f1bd56978

51. Estrem, Pauline. "Why Failure Is Good for Success" (*Success;* August 25, 2016) www.success.com/article/why-failure-is-good-for-success

52. Casner, Steve. "Dumbing It Down in the Cockpit" *Future Tense: The Citizen's Guide to the Future* (Slate, New America, and ASU, December 12, 2014) www.slate.com/articles/technology/future_tense/2014/12/automation_in_the_cockpit_is_making_pilots_thinking_skills_duller.html

53. Ibid.

54. Mills-Scofield, Deborah. "Let's Bring Back Accountability" (*Harvard Business Review*, July 30, 2012) https://hbr.org/2012/07/lets-bring-back-accountability

55. Kavazovic, Ogi. "Dear PMs, It's Time to Rethink Agile at Enterprise Startups" (*First Round Review*) firstround.com/review/dear-pms-its-time-to-rethink-agile-at-enterprise-startups/

56. Ibid.

57. Mitchell, Kip. "Product Debt" (*Inside Axure, Software Development;* March 16, 2017) www.axure.com/blog/product-debt/

58. Stampler, Laura. "CEO Dads Open Up About Balancing Fatherhood and Work" (*TIME;* Living-Families; September 15, 2014) time.com/3342431/work-life-balance-fatherhood-ceos/

59. Clark, James. "52 Inspiring Buddhist Quotes and Sayings on Life" (*Digital Nomad;* Longerm Travel; Nomadic Notes; December 29, 2010) www.nomadicnotes.com/52-inspiring-buddhist-quotes-and-sayings-on-life/

60. Popova, Maria. "Ever Rethinking the Lord's Prayer: Buckminster Fuller Revises Scripture with Science" (*Brain Pickings;* July 12, 2013) www.brainpickings.org/2013/07/12/buckminster-fuller-ever-rethinking-the-Lords-prayer/

61. Definition of Mastery. (The Renaissance Mastery Model. MerriamWebster.com 2016) www.merriam-webster.com/dictionary/mastery

62. Holley, Tiffany. "What Is an Adrenaline Rush?" (*healthfully.com*) healthfully.com/what-adrenaline-rush-5014590.html

63. Esfahani Smith, Emily. "There's More to Life than Being Happy" (*The Atlantic,* January 9, 2013) www.theatlantic.com/health/archive/2013/01/theres-more-to-life-than-being-happy/266805/

64. Ibid.

65. Ibid.

66. Solomon, Micah. "Entrepreneurs: Should You Quit Your Day Job? We Ask *Shark Tank*'s Daymond John" (*Inc;* June 29, 2015) www.inc.com/micah-solomon/when-should-an-entrepreneur-quit-their-day-job-shark-tank-s-daymond-john-has-the.html

67. Chua, Amy. *Battle Hymn of the Tiger Mother* (Penguin, Reprint Edition; December 27, 2011) Pg. 60

68. Hamblin, James. "Buy Experiences, Not Things" (*The Atlantic,* October 7, 2014) www.theatlantic.com/business/archive/2014/10/buy-experiences/381132/

69. Black, John. "Immortality, the Elixir of Life and the Food of the Gods" (*Ancient Origins: Reconstructing the Story of Humanity's Past;* January 6, 2014) www.ancient-origins.net/myths-legends/immortality-elixir-life-and-food-gods-001201

70. Rampell, Catherine. "Planned Obsolescence as Myth or Reality" (*New York Times,* October 31, 2013) economix.blogs.nytimes.com/2013/10/31/planned-obsolescence-as-myth-or-reality

71. Smith, Lisa. "The Disposable Society: An Expensive Place to Live" (*Investopedia*) www.investopedia.com/articles/pf/07/disposablesociety.asp

72. Ayers, Brittany. "A Throw Away Society" (*RCL and Civic Issues Blog – Penn State;* February 6, 2014) www.sites.psu.edu/brittanyblogs20132014/2014/02/06/a-throw-away-society/

73. Dolan, Kerry A. "Garbage: A Costly American Addiction" (*Forbes,* April 13, 2012) www.forbes.com/sites/kerryadolan/2012/04/13/garbage-a-costly-american-addiction/#777503975b1c

74. "Top Green Companies in the U.S. 2016" (*Newsweek;* December 14, 2017) http://www.newsweek.com/green-2016/top-green-companies-us-2016

75. Nygaard, David F. "World Population Projections 2020: A 2020 Vision for Food, Agriculture, and the Environment" (*IFPRI E-Brary Knowledge Repository;* October 1994) core.ac.uk/download/pdf/6242100.pdf

76. Freelich, Amanda. "The Man Who Lives without Money" (*True Activist;* October 21, 2013) www.trueactivist.com/the-man-who-lives-without-money/

77. Ibid.

78. www.eileenfisherlifework.com

79. Smith, Lisa. "The Disposable Society: An Expensive Place to Live" (*Investopedia*) www.investopedia.com/articles/pf/07/disposablesociety.asp

80. KPMG *The Entrée* – Video Episode "Building a Business with Purpose" advisory.kpmg.us/topics/the-entree/building-business-with-purpose.html

81. Ibid.

82. Ibid.

83. Ibid.

84. Moore, Kristina. "Designer Spotlight: Cuyana #fewerbetter" (*Forbes,* November 10, 2015) www.forbes.com/sites/forbesstylefile/2015/11/10/designer-spotlight-cuyana-fewerbetter/#5fb8c5156698

85. Ibid.

86. Ibid.

87. Lampard, Natasha "The Pastry Box Project" (March 27, 2015) the-pastry-box-project.net/natasha-lampard/2015-march-27

88. Ibid.

89. Ibid.

90. *The Rabbit and the Turtle (The New Version)* (YouTube Video; 2012) www.youtube.com/watch?v=GXTeFa43730

91. Radford, Benjamin. "Synchronicity: Definition and Meaning" (*Live Science,* February 4, 2014) www.livescience.com/43105-synchronicity-definition-meaning.html

92. *Design & Thinking* (Film documentary; Yuhsiu Yang; October 3, 2012)

93. Dewey, Benjamin. "Planned Serendipity" (Copyright 2005, *SelfGrowth.com; The Online Self Improvement Community*) www.selfgrowth.com/articles/planned_serendipity.html

94. Heller Zaimont, Rachel. "A Year after the Boston Marathon Bombing, One Victim's Inspiring Startup-Business Story" (*Fast Company;* April 9, 2014) www.fastcompany.com/3028804/a-year-after-the-boston-bombing-one-victims-inspiring-startup-business-story

95. www.unique-design.net/library/word/sense.html

Namaste | www.mellim.com